"THE PERSPECTIVE"

LIBEL

AND THE TEN RULES OF
90'S JOURNALISM

DR. HAROLD BAYS

WE WANT TO HEAR FROM YOU !

If you have any comments, or if you have had a similar experience with the press, please send us a short note to:

Blue Shoes Publishing Inc.

P.O. Box 20968

Louisville Ky. 40250-0968

Library of Congress Cataloging - in - Publication Data

Bays, Harold 1958 -

"The Perspective," Libel, and the Ten Rules of 90's Journalism - or - Medicine, Music, Stand-Up Comedy, Janitor Work, and the Systematic Dismantling of Individual Liberties by an Irresponsible Press

Library of Congress Catalog Card Number: 95 - 78352

Hardcover Trade ISBN 0-9647944-0-3

Softcover Trade ISBN 0-9647944-1-1

Dedication

This book is dedicated to the many honorable journalists who routinely demonstrate, in their reporting, their belief that it is the dedication to protecting individual liberties through reporting *the truth* that defines journalism as a profession. It is my hope that the influence of these dedicated protectors of liberty will grow, such that one day, all of those in the press will realize the importance of truth. It is my hope that all of those in the press will someday appreciate that "The Declaration of Independence" intended that *all* citizens should be given the freedom towards "the pursuit of happiness," without fear or oppression by dictatorships, and that "The Bill of Rights" outlined specific individual liberties that *all* citizens should be granted, without fear or oppression by institutions.

Most importantly, this book is dedicated to the countless citizens, and their families, whose lives have been tragically altered, and whose individual rights have been arrogantly ignored when dealing with an irresponsible press. It is sobering to find that the very Constitution that was to have protected individual rights, has been contorted to grant the press the legal loophole to dismantle individual liberties - without reasonable recourse.

Believe me. I know.

For the sake of journalism, and for the sake of individual liberties, this needs to stop.

BILL OF RIGHTS

AMENDMENT (1) - Congress shall make no law respecting an establishment of religion, or prohibiting the free exercise thereof; or abridging the freedom of speech, or of the press; or the right of the people peaceably to assemble, and to petition the government for a redress of grievances.

AMENDMENT (2) - A well regulated Militia, being necessary to the security of a free State, the right of the people to keep and bear Arms, shall not be infringed.

AMENDMENT (3) - No soldier shall, in times of peace be quartered in any house, without the consent of the Owner, nor in the time of war, but in a manner to be prescribed by law.

AMENDMENT (4) - The right of the people to be secure in their person, houses, paper, and effects, against unreasonable searches and seizures, shall not be violated, and no Warrants shall issue but upon probable cause, supported by Oath or affirmation, and particularly describing the place to be searched, and the persons or things to be seized.

AMENDMENT (5) - No person shall be held answer for a capital, or otherwise infamous crime, unless on a presentment or indictment of a grand jury, except in cases arising in the land or Naval forces, or in the Militia, when in actual service in time of war or public danger; nor shall any person be subject for the same offense to be twice put in jeopardy of life or limb; or shall be compelled in any criminal case to be a witness against himself, or be deprived of life, liberty, or property, without due process of law; nor shall private property be taken for public use, without just compensation.

AMENDMENT (6) - In all criminal prosecutions, the accused shall enjoy the right to a speedy and public trial, by an impartial jury of the state and district wherein the crime shall have been committed, which district shall had been previously ascertained by law, and to be informed of the nature and cause of the accusation; to be confronted with the witness against him; to have compulsory process for obtaining witnesses in his favor, and to have the Assistance of Counsel for his defense.

AMENDMENT (7) - In Suits at common law where the value and controversy shall exceed $20.00 dollars, the right of trial by jury shall be preserved, and no fact try to jury, shall be otherwise reexamined in a Court of the United States, than according the rules of the common law.

AMENDMENT (8) - Excessive bail shall not be required, nor excessive fines imposed, nor cruel and unusual punishment inflicted.

AMENDMENT (9) - The enumeration in the Constitution, of certain rights, shall not be construed to deny or disparage others retained by the people.

AMENDMENT (10) - The powers not delegated to the United States by Constitution, nor prohibited it to the States, are reserved to the States respectively, or to the people.

AMENDMENT (14) - All person born or naturalized in the United States and subject to the jurisdiction thereof, are citizens of the United States and of the state wherein they reside. No state shall make or enforce any law which shall abridge the privileges or immunities of citizens of the United Sttes; nor shall any state deprive any person of life, liberty, or property, without due process of law; nor deny to any person within its jurisdiction the equal protection of the laws.

Special Thanks

To my wife Dawn, who I hope someday will quit having to listen to, "Why do you work, your husband's a doctor?"

To the rest of my family and in-laws who stuck by me during this ordeal.

And to my son Jason. May he live in a world in which the press better fulfills its Constitutional obligation to help protect and honor his individual liberties.

Disclaimer

I am not an attorney. The enclosed information and recommendations are my opinion based on my experience. For legal advice, contact an attorney.

CONTENTS

FOREWORD

Most folks feel that America's greatness, in no small way, is founded in the steadfast defense of the individual rights of its citizens. In the First Amendment of the Bill of Rights, the press is given the constitutional obligation to protect these individual liberties.

And it is the dedication to protecting individual liberties through reporting the truth that defines journalism as a profession.

Unfortunately, too many journalists have forgotten this basic obligation.

The author, Dr. Harold Bays, a Kentucky physician, describes how a Gannett newspaper deliberately, and with malice, harmed his reputation and family in a significantly fabricated, front-page, lead headline story of the day.

His incredible journey to seek justice was thwarted at each step of the way, offering a real-life example of how it was not suppose to be.

It was through his observation and experience that he established,

"The Ten Rules of 90's Journalism."

Any citizen who is respected in the community, who is in a position of authority, or who is simply successful needs to understand these rules. Because today, tomorrow, or at anytime in the future, Dr. Bays' ordeal demonstrates that anyone is a potential target for the "perspective" of an irresponsible reporter.

No one is immune. No one is safe.

To those who have been libeled, this book will clarify the reasonable options available to achieve justice, as well as the potential futility in appealing to a libelous press with pleas of decency and fairness.

To those who advise clients who may have been libeled, (lawyers, press-relations firms, etc.) this book will clarify why "no comment" is often the best response to any accusation by the press, no matter how wrong, how old, or how outlandish the claim.

But most of all, to those of us who are just regular folks, this book will clarify how powerless citizens are in achieving justice when confronted with the absolute power of the multibillion dollar press industry.

CHAPTER I:

THIS CAN'T BE HAPPENING

"Denial, anger, acceptance."

MEDICINE

Denial.

Anger.

Acceptance.

Patients who have had a face-to-face encounter with impending death may go through these emotional phases. But these phases are not always exclusive to death. Similar emotions may apply to other life events as well.

Much of my physician training took place at a Veterans Administration (VA) Hospital. Those who advocate nationalized health care should spend some time in a VA Hospital. This is an excellent model of how a current U.S. government-run, medical delivery system operates.

And as bad as the current, private medical system may seem, government run health care has its own problems.

First of all, to say that the treatment at VA Hospitals has sometimes lagged behind private hospitals is an understatement. Without going into detail, suffice it to say some have referred to the VA Hospital as:

"The hospital that time forgot."

4

It is illustrative to note that, during my training, the VA cafeteria was still called "The Canteen." And the food was exactly what one would expect from any eating establishment called,

"The Canteen."

I can remember countless evenings on call when my colleagues and I would be up until 3:00 AM in the morning taking care of critically ill veterans. But regardless of the lack of sleep, we always would arrive promptly at 6:00 AM to make it to "The Canteen" on time. This was not because we were hungry. We simply wanted to see what sort of diabolical pentagon experiment they were serving that day.

For example, on one particular Sunday morning, one of the menu items was the "omelet surprise." Being a curious, and a notably fearless medical resident, I bravely ordered the "omelet surprise." I was subsequently handed a stainless steel plate with a yellow plastic cover. Upon pulling off the plastic cover, the enigmatic "omelet surprise" was revealed.

It was a hot dog wrapped in an egg.

At 6 AM in the morning.

Denial.

As I peered at the "omelet surprise" in disbelief, the cook seemed annoyed and bluntly stated,

"You got a problem with that son."

5

Anger.

> "Oh, no," I said.

> "I'm just thinking of what would make this dining experience complete. Suddenly, I thought how wonderful it would be if we had some of yesterday's Spam souffle to accompany this exquisite cuisine."

Acceptance.

In fairness, it should be stated that VA hospitals are not unique in slow-to-change bureaucracies. Cumbersome stagnation is a not unexpected consequence of many government-run programs. But the VA is certainly a reasonable illustration of a clunky program, designed by well-meaning people, that often becomes contorted by self-serving abuses.

For example, when I was a medical student, the VA Hospital was paid per bed occupied. Therefore, the admission policy was, shall we say, "liberal." It was not uncommon for patients with stable stroke or Alzheimer's disease to be admitted for "nursing home placement." Such patients were not admitted for any particular hospital emergency. Rather, these demented, but medically stable patients were admitted for the sole purpose of filling beds, and were sometimes hospitalized for weeks to months. To make matters worse, some of these medically stable patients would be placed on wards, surrounded by ill and contagious patients as they waited placement.

Therefore, although a skilled care facility or nursing home may have provided more appropriate care, there was no (economic) incentive to expedite this process.

Because the more the beds were filled, the more money was granted to the VA hospital, regardless of the patients' health.

In another example, most any doctor who trained at a VA hospital during the 1980's can relate to the substantial delays of simple tests such as blood tests and X-ray studies. The longer the delay of obtaining diagnostic tests, the longer the patient went without diagnosis and treatment, and the longer the patients stayed in the hospital. And because each veteran patient was assigned to a medical "team," these delays often resulted in very large numbers of patients per team. And the more patients that mounted up on each team, the more patients were in the hospital.

And the more the beds were filled, the more money was granted to the VA hospital, regardless of the patients' health.

Sometimes the patient load became overwhelming. There-fore, the more crafty leaders of medical teams developed ingenious ways to try and beat the system. Some residents were known to initially order a barrage of diagnostic studies for each admitted patient, irrespective of the medical need. This would, in effect, reserve a diagnostic testing "slot" for the medical team. If it was determined that any of these tests were not required for the current patient, then the scheduled diagnostic test "slot" would be held and used for future patients on this team. In this way, diagnostic studies would be saved up and used to expedite the care and diagnosis of the patients. Furthermore, it would expedite the discharge of patients from this team, and thus the patient load would be decreased. This would allow the doctors to spend more time focusing on patients that truly required hospitalization.

This is an example of the twisted efforts, and the bureaucratic gymnastics that must sometimes occur in order to achieve some degree of practical efficiency in U.S. government-run programs.

And to be clear, no one questions the facts that many veterans have benefited, and are entitled to care given through VA Hospitals. In my judgement, the promise of medical care to veterans was a covenant between the government and anyone who placed their life on the line for America. But even the most ardent VA supporters would admit that there is widespread abuse of the system. Although it is politically impossible for the politicians to admit, let me drop a bombshell:

> Some veterans (who may have never fought a battle in their life) abuse the VA system.

And the abuse is far more common than the public can imagine. Every medical resident who has worked at a VA has his/her favorite "abuse of the system" story.

I have several.

For example, I use to moonlight at the VA Hospital Emergency Room. One evening I was called by the nurse who stated that a patient had come in for an "emergency" at 3:00 AM in the morning. I arose from my cot, walked down the hall to the ER treatment area, and found an obviously intoxicated 30-something man. He was requesting a hospital bed because it was Derby Week in Louisville, Kentucky, and he needed a place to stay.

"This can't be happening," I thought.

Denial.

I explained that he had entered a VA Hospital designed for sick veterans, not a VA Hilton for intoxicated former file clerks who needed a place to crash during Derby week. He seemed somewhat surprised and agitated at my suggestion that he required an illness to be admitted to the hospital.

"Well wonder if I told you I had severe knee pain?" he inquired.

I explained that knee pain would not typically warrant admission to a hospital.

"Well wonder if I told you I had a bad cough?" he hacked.

I explained that unless the cough was associated with a severe illness, then again, hospitalization would not be indicated.

"Well, wonder if I told you I just took 42 Valiums in an attempt to kill myself?!"

"Welcome to the VA Hilton," I replied.

Anger.

Although it was clear I was being manipulated, I was required to take his statement seriously. With a wry, and conquering smile, he watched me fill out the admission papers as I contacted the medical team to inform them of this admission of an attempted suicide, and drug overdose.

After arranging for his admission, it was my responsibility to lavage his gastric contents. I am not certain as to the origin of the word "lavage." I suspect it is a French term that may stand for,

> "Wash your guts out."

Basically, a gastric lavage is a procedure in which a large bore plastic/rubber tube is inserted through the nostril, through the esophagus, and into the stomach. Subsequently, fluid is infused through the tube into the stomach, and then drained into a basin. The purpose of this procedure is to "wash" out any remaining pills that had not as yet been absorbed or passed into the gastrointestinal tract. As I approached this patient with the large bore plastic/rubber tube, he replied,

> "What the hell are you going to do with
> that?"

I then explained the procedure of the gastric lavage. I explained that I would take this large bore plastic/rubber tube insert it through his nostril, through his esophagus and into the stomach in order to help drain his gastric contents.

> "The hell you are!"

He then tried to convince me that he had not taken the valiums, and merely said so because he needed a place to stay for Derby. But I was medically obligated to complete my evaluation and treatment. I could not simply attribute his intoxicated state solely to alcohol. I could not simply disregard his prior confession of an overdose attempt. And although it would have been much simpler, and much more desirable to forego my medical responsibilities, I had an ethical obligation to proceed with the gastric lavage procedure in an attempt to potentially save a life.

As might be expected, the patient was somewhat resistant to this procedure. He became combative. Numerous security guards were required to restrain and stabilize the patient as the large bore plastic/rubber tube was inserted through the nose, through the esophagus, and into the stomach.

As he thrashed back and forth, blood tinged mucous sprayed about the room from his fiery nostrils. And amongst this fight and furry, there became a sudden telling moment that will forever be etched upon my mind. Near the very end of this procedure, he suddenly stopped his cursing and thrashing, looked me straight into the eye and said,

> "I bet you're lovin' this, aren't you?"

This was a telling moment that vividly demonstrated the level of understanding of those who just don't have a clue.

As a professional, I of course denied gathering any enjoyment from the gastric lavage procedure. However, because of the ridiculousness of his question, I must admit a part of me would rather have responded with:

> "You know, you are exactly right. Before you came in, I was lying on the cot in the

11

back room trying to think of what would
make my emergency room experience complete. Suddenly, I thought how wonderful it
would be if I could wash out some obnoxious
drunk's stomach, and drain his partially
digested Denny's Big Breakfast on my
shoes."

"That would really make my night complete."

"Then you came in. What are the odds?"

"By the way, how was the omelet surprise?"

Acceptance.

The point is, adverse life events are often associated with
denial, anger, and acceptance.

And medical training imparts a knowledge through
experiences that can be found in no other profession.

It is a blessing to have the mental ability to absorb the
enormous factual knowledge required in understanding
disease and treatment. It is a sacrifice to forego years,
friends, and family in the quest towards achieving the ability
to heal. And it is almost a spiritual awakening to witness
how this acquired knowledge and human ability saves lives.

But sometimes, the lessons come harder than expected.

During my third year as a medical resident, the VA
intensive care units were undergoing renovations. But rather
than transferring intensively ill patients to other hospitals
with real intensive care units (which would cost the VA
money), regular patient's rooms were converted into

make-shift intensive care beds.

The more the beds were filled, the more money was granted to the VA hospital, regardless of the patients' health.

I was in charge of one of the medical teams on call at the VA Hospital. "Being on call" meant that any patient who came to the Emergency Room with an illness that required hospitalization would be admitted to me, and thus, to my team. My team consisted of first year medical interns, medical students, and sometimes oral surgeons. Although having oral surgeons on a medical team may seem odd, it was a requirement of their training that they receive one year of internal medicine experience before proceeding on with completion of their oral surgery training.

(They were not, however, expected to perform emergency flossing, or other such urgent dental procedures).

On one particular evening, I was called to see an intensive care unit patient (of another medical team that was not on call) in one of the make-shift intensive care rooms. His medical health was deteriorating. In review of the chart, the patient had a long history of diabetes, had undergone bilateral above-the-knee amputations, and had experienced several heart attacks.

He was terminal.

Throughout the evening, his blood pressure continued to drop to critical levels, despite the intensive care nurses' best effort. On entering the room, there was an eerie 2:00

AM darkness as the cold rain lightly tapped upon the windows that surrounded his bed. The monitors that had been brought into this make shift-room were stacked directly above his head. The patient was intubated and had multiple tubes that entered into his body, and multiple wires taped onto his body that served to connect him to the numerous machines monitoring his vital signs. The only noise in the room was the light hum of the intravenous pumps, and the faint beep of the EKG monitor that displayed a brilliant, fluorescent green heart tracing - that visually peaked in synchrony with the auditory beeps - that in turn, echoed the beat of his heart.

The patient was alert.

After an evaluation of the clinical data, and a quick physical exam, I surmised that this man's heart was rapidly failing and that his lungs would soon fill with fluid resulting in eventual death by suffocation and asphyxiation.

Saving his life was now my responsibility.

In the pre-clinical, regimented medical school years, my academic performance was average. Sitting in a classroom, and being required to listen to lectures made me nervous. However, once I entered into the clinical 3rd year and beyond, I was allowed to study on my own without being required to attend lectures. My academic performance vastly improved. By the time I was a medical resident, I had been awarded for achieving the highest scores on the in-house service exams. And, I would eventually go on to score in the top 20% of the nation on my Internal Medicine Boards, as well as achieve other academic honors. In the midst of this academic success, I became proud and protective of my medical performance.

Prior to this patient, my record was spotless in that no patient had ever died in the hospital while directly under my medical care. Although I had been criticized by my colleagues for my aggressiveness in saving the lives of otherwise terminal patients, it was my feeling that the only way I could gain the knowledge and the expertise of saving lives was to go all out to save lives during my training. I felt I had plenty of time later on in my medical career to learn when and how to let patients die.

But now I was faced with a patient who was rapidly worsening, despite my best efforts. This was a direct challenge to my abilities, and a challenge to my "record."

Denial.

As I leaned my back against the midnight window several feet from the patient, I evaluated and re-evaluated all potential modes of treatment. But despite the manipulation and administration of multiple combinations of blood pressure raising medications, his medical condition continued to worsen.

Nevertheless, I persisted with all efforts. Finally, I considered the absurd possibility that a positive mental attitude may be of some help. Although it seems ridiculous now, at 3:00 AM in the morning, it seemed reasonable that if the patient had a positive mental attitude that his condition would improve, perhaps this might assist in his

15

recovery.

At the very least, I wanted to appear positive so as to not to frighten the patient about his impending death. So each time I entered the room, I was upbeat. And I gave him any positive information that truthfully could be told. Although he was intubated and unable to speak, he did nod his head at each suggestion of improvement, as if to agree, and as if to be thankful.

But I was growing increasingly frustrated that my medical abilities were being thwarted by the natural course of death.

Anger.

I am not sure how it happened, but after a few hours of my futile minute to minute bedside efforts, the chaplain arrived at the nurses' station. How and why the chaplain came at such a late hour, I have no idea. Nevertheless, I explained to the chaplain that I was doing everything that I could to medically treat the patient. I explained that I had full confidence that I was doing the right thing from a scientific perspective.

The chaplain then asked if he could see the patient. I thought this was an appropriate decision. Perhaps the presence of a chaplain would further improve the patient's health by letting him know that the "big doc in the sky" was also on his side.

And I explained to the chaplain my theory of keeping a positive mental attitude.

The chaplain then entered the darkened room. The rain

continued to pelt the surrounding windows. He introduced himself to the patient, and began to make small talk. The patient listened with attentiveness. After about 10 minutes, there occurred a sudden telling moment that will forever be etched upon my mind. From somewhere totally out of the blue, and prompted for reasons unknown (at least to me), the chaplain suddenly looked into the eyes of the patient and stated:

"Would you like to pray with me?"

The patient enthusiastically nodded his head.

I was taken totally off guard and was dumbfounded. This was a telling moment that vividly demonstrated the level of understanding of someone who just didn't have a clue (i.e. me).

It was clear that I had not convinced the patient of his well-being - despite all my medical expertise, and despite my "positive attitude" approach. Furthermore, it was clear the chaplain had something far more valuable to offer the patient at this point than my scientific abilities.

I have since learned the lesson that medical science is only a part of healing.

Acceptance.

MUSIC

"Death" is a term that is often applied to situations other than the demise of a human being. In the arts, analogies to death are often used to describe poor performances.

"Man, we died."

New Year's Eve is a benchmark for the success of any musician. Because of the high demand, New Year's Eve gigs are among the easiest to get, and among the highest paying jobs of the year.

I had grown a custom to playing New Year's Eve music jobs yearly with such historically important groups such as The Progress Notes (top 40), Pulsar (country rock), and The Flying Monkeys (jazz and 60s music).

On one fateful New Year's Eve night I was playing with the band "Blue Shoes and the Garden" at a local country club. We were in the midst of a particularly moving passage of the classic "Wang Dang Doodle" when we began to notice that the members of the country club were pointing towards their watches. It was with horror that the guitar player and I discovered that it was only minutes until midnight. The guitar player then looked at the drummer and signaled that our current song be stopped.

The drummer, being a drummer, refused.

Denial.

This is one of the disadvantages of performing in a band who performs without rules. In my experience, bands that engage in stage performances encompass a spectrum between two extremes. In bands dominated by a singer or singers, the song length and notes played are often rigidly determined. The singers know exactly when they are expected to sing, the musicians know exactly what they are expected to play, and the entire band knows exactly how to start and how to end each song. Although some of the creativity may be lost, the professionalism and the "slickness" of the band is markedly enhanced.

Alternatively, I more often played in bands that were less rigid. Before each song, we rarely knew how the tune would be played, nor who would play what or when. And we sure didn't know how the tune would end.

Because I began my music career reading music, it would seem that I would have been more comfortable with a sheet-music mentality. But my beginnings as a paid musician were quite unlike my grade school, high school and college academic musical background.

I was raised in a town in southern Kentucky. Although it has grown considerably since, in my youth, we basically had one mall, two family restaurants (a Pizza Hut and a Bonanza), and a McDonald's. But whileas eating establishments were limited, there were no shortages of bars and nightclubs. Among my first experiences with breaking into the music scene was when my friend T.L. (trumpet prodigy and now Vice President and Financial Analyst for a major investment firm) took me to the "Camelot Pickin' Parlor." This was a run down building with a stage and sound system. On certain nights of the week, any musician (of any age) could "sit in" and play for the long-haired 60's audience who would sit on the floor and applaud and appreciate just about anything. It was an excellent opportunity to gain experience as a performing musician.

And being an aspiring musician in southern Kentucky did have its geographical advantages. My hometown was approximately 60 miles away from Nashville, Tennessee. Because of the abundance of musicians, and because only the very best of the best musicians held steady gigs in Nashville proper, many other excellent musicians would try to find work in surrounding areas and towns. Therefore, due to the overflow of supply, it was often cheaper for nightclub owners to hire a live band than to pay a D.J. to play pre-recorded tapes and records. For that reason, it was not uncommon to go to the local pizza restaurant at midnight and find a five piece, incredible blue-grass band playing on a 7 by 7 foot stage.

This kind of music environment was instrumental towards gaining experience as a performing musician.

After moving to Louisville Ky. to go to medical school, I went from band to band with my "axe" (saxophone). It was during residency that I joined "Blue Shoes in the Garden."

It was this band that was playing this New Year's gig.

It was now approximately 12:01 AM. The country club audience was obviously getting nervous that we had not completed our "Wang Dang Doodle." Despite the guitar player's best efforts, the drummer refused to yield.

Finally, the guitarist directly, sternly, but respectfully requested that the drummer cease. His request was colored with precisely chosen expletives designed to impart the immediate nature of his petition. The drummer responded (as would be expected of most drummers) by throwing his sticks on the floor and walking off the stage.

Anger.

The keyboard player could not believe this was happening. The guitar player was angry. And I just was thankful that the drummer had not broken the guitar-player's teeth with his drum sticks - again.

Acceptance.

Being accustomed to the quaint, "devil-may-care" attitude of drummers, the guitar player and I, without missing a beat, (although we clearly were missing an auditory beat), handled the situation, We counted off,

> "Five - four - three - two - one - Happy
> New Year."

We then began to play a most unfortunate version of Auld Lang Syne. Nevertheless, we had met a deadline head on and were able to meet our obligation in a responsible manner.

21

STAND-UP COMEDY

As with any warrior on the front lines, stand-up comics often share war stories.

Tales of victory usually fall on deaf ears, because they are often overstated, or simply represent a telling moment that vividly demonstrates the level of understanding of an unsuccessful comic who does not have a clue about his or her competence.

Conversely, tales of comedy death are always believed.

And I believe that I may hold the record of undergoing one of the worst comedy deaths of all time.

I was traveling down I-65 in my 1975 blue Monte Carlo equipped with the standard equipment of dented fenders, slashed and worn through seats, dash console devoid of radio, cracked front windshield, speedometer with 150,000 miles, and big pair of fuzzy dice dangling on the rear view mirror.

This was one loaded automobile.

It also had a rain roof.

A sun roof has a large windowed opening in the roof of the

car that allows the light from the sun to enter into the car.

A moon roof has a smaller windowed opening in the roof of the car that allows moonlight to enter into the car

A rain roof has many much smaller openings, usually as the result of rust, that allows the rain to come into the car.

My Monte Carlo had a rain roof.

(A few years later, my "blues mobile" or "blue bomb" suddenly underwent multi-organ failure requiring an immediate detour off the expressway to Budget-Rent-A-Car, wherein I purchased my current 1987 Grand Am on the spot).

On my way down I-65 to a comedy job in a small town in Tennessee, I had just come off of several successful comedy gigs. I had so much success, that I began to compare myself with national comics.

Hence, I had made the classic mistake of the performing arts. In thinking that past successes insured at least adequate future performances, I was setting myself up for doom.

Denial.

My first clue that something was awry was when, upon arriving at the club, I asked the club owner if any of the kids from the college, just three blocks away, typically came to the club.

He seemed confused.

I'm not sure he knew a college existed, or perhaps what the word "college" meant. And in viewing the clientele in the bar, it was clear that not only did he not know, but he obviously did not care. Located within the club were an assortment of buzz-headed hooligans who are quite content in entertaining themselves with pitchers of beer, explicit language, and deafening screams that were reminiscent of the frightening "rebel yell" of years gone by.

To my horror, I began to realize that the nuances of stand up comedy were the last thing on their minds.

The disc jockey then took the stage to start the show. As with many D.J.'s, he was kind of a pitiful human being. It was his job to announce the comics and "warm up" the crowd. But even though it was a minor part of the show, it was however, a golden opportunity for him to be the center of attention. Being granted a stage and forum that forced others to listen to his gibberish was a dream come true.

And it cost a lot less than therapy.

And after witnessing his feeble attempts at comedy, it became clear why his real job entailed sitting alone in a booth playing the recordings of talented persons.

The opening comic then hit the stage. He electrified the audience with a series of re-tread fat-guy jokes complete with the pre-requisite explicit language. His ending, killer "bit" had something to do with a water slide enema.

The audience roared with appreciation.

He had reached their level of understanding.

The D.J. then re-took the stage. He again made several feeble attempts at being humorous, all of which again failed. But to his credit he again "warmed up" the crowd by requesting that the audience chant with what appeared to be a ritual within the club. He would start by saying,

"Attitude check. What do you say?"

And in reply, the audience would scream back,

"F _ _ K YOU!"

Ain't that America?

This was repeated several times. And at the peak of the barbarism, the DJ then read my introduction as,

"And now, please welcome sociopolitical commentary of Dr. Harold Bays."

Being initiated into a fraternity in college, I thought I knew the meaning of hazing. Even in medical school, it is tradition that medical students are ridiculed ("hazed") as idiots and slackers, regardless of their efforts, and regardless of their academic backgrounds.

For example, as a Junior in medical school during a noon conference for the hospital staff, I was required to present an educational surgical case regarding a patient I had never met. The Attending surgeon who performed the case, and with whom I had never worked with, began to ruthlessly grill me about the specific aspects of the patient's history and surgical treatment, much of which were in records that were never provided to me.

As I stood helplessly lost at the podium, he and the other surgeons were circling like sharks. The more I bled, the hungrier they became. And it became clear that any self respect I had achieved in a lifetime of academic success would not be re-affirmed today. And as they continued to rail upon me, I had an out-of-body experience.

A part of my mind went on autopilot. This reflex part of my mind allowed my mouth to continue to respond to the inquisition without much cognitive effort. But the aware-ness, out-of-body part of my mind allowed me to observe the crowd witnessing this debacle. And as I looked in their eyes, there became a sudden, telling moment that will forever be etched upon my mind.

On one hand, I saw a look of horror, sympathetic that no human being should be treated in such an unfair and disrespectful manner. But on the other hand, I saw in those same eyes an unmistakable gladness that they were there to see it.

Weren't they there when David met the lions?

I envisioned that these were the same people that bring traffic to a screeching halt as they slow down to try and see auto fatalities on the side of the road.

So I thought I knew hazing.

But I was totally unprepared for what occurred in that small town in Tennessee.

Anger.

I never had a chance. From the beginning, the audience had absolutely no interest in what was occurring on stage. They threw expletives at each other in an almost Klingon dialect, threw their beers down their guts, and then threw quarters at the stage.

At first I could not believe this was happening (denial). But my denial turned to anger when the audience refused to yield. In desperation, I asked the only three people listening on the front row what was going on. They stated quite simply,

"It ain't pretty."

However, it was my job to stay on stage for 30 minutes. But I was in a quandary. How could I entertain these heathens? The audience had no interest in comedy, and certainly had no interest in sociopolitical issues. Therefore, I began to look to find ways to occupy their time. For example, one member of the crowd, for no particular reason, suddenly screamed non-stop for about 30 seconds, I then saw a golden opportunity. I immediately started a contest to see who could scream the loudest and longest. The winner was a young man who, upon rearing his head back and screaming to the point of literal unconsciousness, passed out and fell backwards over his chair.

He may have been a drunken fool to most people.

But he was a hero to his peers.

Even years afterwards, my comedy colleagues know this as one of the worst comedy experiences of all time. Nevertheless, I did my 30 minutes. Although more painful than can ever be told, I fulfilled my responsibility.

Acceptance.

JANITOR WORK

Much has been written about the government's role in providing safety in the workplace. But some work activity requires risk that is inherent in the job. Other work risk is the result of stupid things that are done by employees, so bizarre as to circumvent all attempts at prevention.

When cooking steaks on a broiler, the grease is not only drained into grease pans, but also is aerosolized towards the cooks. At the end of a long evening of cooking T-bones and sirloins, my face and skin would be caked with a thick film of what was akin to a petroleum by-product.

Some environmental hazards just come with the job.

After work, in order to unclog our skin pores with sweat, we would often go to a local church. There, glowing in the concrete parking lot at midnight, would be what in Kentucky is often considered a religious shrine - a basketball goal. Hence, equipped with the standard uniform of black work shoes, white socks, blue work pants, and white shirts, we would play basketball for hours.

And sweat.

Ain't that America?

28

It was a sorrowful day indeed when one evening after work, we found the church had torn the goal down. We will never know the real reason. Oh sure, the church issued some lame excuse. They said that the goal had to go because rednecks were playing basketball at all hours of the night. This was of course a fabrication, because as stated before, we were there most every evening.

And we never saw any rednecks.

Denial.

After basketball, I would return to the restaurant to begin my janitor work. On one particular evening, we had the honor of entertaining members of a notable motorcycle organization. The manner in which they left the restaurant was unkind.

What was done to the carpet was objectionable. What was done to the salad bar was offensive. But what was done to the bathrooms was almost criminal.

And that I was the janitor that evening was most unfortunate.

Anger.

After vacuuming the floors, mopping up the condiments, and utilizing my janitorial skills on urinals and toilets, I then proceeded to the tiled floors in the grilling area. It was then that I decided to use a unique cleaning technique developed by a coworker and myself. We had developed a janitorial breakthrough when encountering especially dirty and greasy floors.

First I mopped the floor with a generous dose of clorox. This was followed by a hefty helping of ammonia. A wonderful, cleansing mixture was created, accompanied by a dry-ice appearing, mystical, whitish fog.

I would later learn that this was probably chlorine gas. This would certainly explain why I found it so difficult to breathe when using this potion.

Some environmental hazards just come with the stupidity.

Acceptance.

CHAPTER 2:

THIS CAN'T BE HAPPENING TO ME

"After all, I felt that journalists were
basically good, decent, hard working people
trying to do a job that had constitutional
purpose and merit. Furthermore, since I had
faith that reporters and editors had an
uncompromising dedication to truth, and an
unyielding respect and compassion for the
reputation of the very citizens they had a
constitutional obligation to protect, I felt my
willingness to cooperate would ensure
accuracy and fairness."

NAIVETE

I had held many jobs and had encountered many obstacles. Because of my diverse life experiences, I considered myself a reasonably aware person. And although my prior interactions with the press had been limited, I thought myself accurate in my perception that journalism was a most virtuous profession.

And it remains true today that many folks, particularly from smaller towns, generally feel the press is composed of decent, hard-working people with the highest level of integrity. From time to time, folks may disagree with the political editorials. But when it comes to reporting the news, most folks have faith that reporters and editors have an uncompromising dedication to truth, and have an unyielding respect and compassion for the reputation of the very citizens they have a constitutional obligation to protect.

For example, if an allegation is reported against one of our neighbors, it is generally believed that painstaking journalistic efforts were made to insure accuracy and balance to protect the accused's reputation, family and friends. The concept of "innocent until proven guilty" is not just a judicial concept, it represents a common decency we all share. Everyone is entitled to fairness during trial by jury. And, likewise, no one should have their individual liberties compromised during trial by the press.

Because it is the dedication to protecting individual liberties through reporting the truth that defines journalism as a profession.

Before May of 1994, I shared this view. It was a mystery to me as to why citizens accused of wrongdoing were so often advised by "experts" to make "no comment," rather than to simply cooperate with the press. After all, the only interest of the press was to report the truth. And it seemed intuitively obvious that if one was innocent, then the truth would be told, and the innocent would surely be portrayed as innocent.

But *since* May 1994, my view has changed. For those who know the press to be irresponsible, the following will only confirm this knowledge. For those who had the highest respect for the profession of journalism (as did I), the following may provide insight as to why public skepticism of the press is leading to cynicism. And as these events are read, it should be remembered:

If this happened to me, it could happen to anyone.

It could happen to you.

THE BACKGROUND

I grew up in southern Kentucky. At age 14, I began working
20 - 40 hours a week as a busboy at one of the (then) only
two family restaurants in town - Bonanza Sirloin Pit. My
hard work and dedication paid off as I steadily advanced to
dishwasher, fry man, bread man, set-up man, and eventually
to cook. After 2 years of being head cook, I reached the
pinnacle of my restaurant career. I achieved the status of
midnight janitor.

Finally, during my last years in college, I was able to make
an upward/lateral corporate jump to becoming a clerk at
Food Mart.

But despite a full work schedule, I was able to achieve
academic success. I became President of the Pre-Medical
College Honor Society, and was accepted "early decision"
at the University of Louisville School of Medicine.

In Medical School, I quickly learned one of the greatest
misconceptions of postgraduate education,

> "You can always borrow as much money as
> you want."

Money problems haunted me throughout my medical

education. My freshman year, I lived in a $125 a month apartment in "Old Louisville." This monthly charge included the costs of an unairconditioned, unheated, single room attached to a bathroom. Located downstairs was a lobby phone, refrigerator, and dining room table shared by all the inhabitants in what was essentially a boarding house.

My neighbors were colorful. Next door was a college student who periodically wore white, para-trooper uniforms. His subscriptions included socialist "We Will Rise Again Against the Capitalist Pigs" magazines. He seemed like a nice guy.

A little different, but nice.

The 60's couple downstairs had no furniture and slept on the floor. I believe they drove a Volkswagen bus.

Because my maximum yearly loan was around $7500, with approximately $2500 going for books and tuition, this left $5000 for room, boarding, and food. It was enough to sustain existence, but it was difficult to afford many living needs. (I did not receive governmental assistance). Consequently, I was often required to leave my 1975 Monte Carlo (with 187,000 miles) parked on the street, while I road my bike and road the city bus to medical school.

Later on, I was able to move across the street to a "carriage house" that was two rooms attached to a bathroom for $165 a month. The mutant roaches and abundant mice inside, as well as the stray and howling alley cats outside, were thrown in for free.

During my residency and fellowship, I began to draw a modest salary. I moonlighted in emergency rooms. I worked virtually every Christmas and Thanksgiving (because the hourly reimbursement was the greatest during the holidays - plus, who could resist those hospital turkey dinners?). With these incomes, and with income from music gigs, I was finally able to afford an apartment that was vermin-free. My academic performance vastly improved. I was awarded for the highest scores on the in-house service exam both my second and third year in internal medicine residency. I scored in the top 1/5th in the nation on my Internal Medicine Examination Boards.

In retrospect, I often wonder where I would have fit on the "Bell Curve."

After two additional years in fellowship, I received my second board certification in Endocrinology and Metabolism. In 1989, I joined a well-established physician group consisting of two Endocrinologists. They were partners; I was an employee.

In 1993, I left this practice to form my own practice with my new associate. She was also an Endocrinologist with an exemplary academic background. And the business practices, the office fees, and the laboratory fees of our current practice bore little relation to my previous practice for which I was simply an employee. And most importantly, because of the dramatic changes in the medical market place due to managed care, fees for most medical services had undergone substantial changes and bore little relation to fees of just 2 years prior.

This should be repeated: Because of the dramatic changes in the medical market place due to managed care, fees for most medical services had undergone substantial changes and bore little relation to fees of just 2 years prior.

And finally, since 1990, I had been the Medical Director of a cholesterol and metabolic research center, conducting Phase II-IV clinical research trials. I had published my research findings and experience in worldwide publications.

I had lived the American Dream. But I had not forgotten how much I owed to a community that has allowed me such an opportunity to achieve. Hence, I had actively been involved in many charitable causes. Furthermore, I had been recognized with honor for my physician volunteer work with the homeless.

The point is, whether it be the advancement of academics, or volunteer efforts to benefit the community, I believe I had made a difference. And until May of 1994, I thought I had truly earned, and rightly deserved, the respect of my neighbors and colleagues.

THE PATIENT

It all began with a forgotten, disgruntled patient (Ms. E.C.), that I had seen over two years prior while I was an employee of a previous medical practice.

Not every doctor has a personality that matches every patient. And, in the case of Ms. E.C., I was but one of many doctors that she was less than thrilled about. After my medical evaluation, she complained about her bill. This is nothing new. Many people complain about their doctor bills. Many people complain about their car repair bills, attorney bills, electric bills, plumbing bills, cable bills, newspaper advertising bills, etc. In fact, isolated billing complaints routinely occur in virtually every small business.

Doctor bills are no exception.

But while as billing complaints against others can be freely and openly justified, doctors are often limited in their ability to openly discuss the justification of charges due to issues of patient confidentiality. Many issues have yet to be fully disclosed, even today. Nevertheless, even after Ms. E.C. voluntarily released any and all aspects of her medical care to the press, I have limited my comments only to those issues that I feel necessary to correct wrongful accusations.

And to be honest, Ms. E.C. played only a minor role in prompting this book.

On February 2, 1992, while as an employee of a previous medical practice, I initially saw Ms. E.C. She was a 57 year old woman who desired to see a thyroid specialist because she did not accept the opinion of numerous other doctors she had seen for the same condition. It would later be reported by a Gannett reporter, that she had a history of repeated problems with doctors. In fact, Gannett would later report that Ms. E.C. "changed doctors as often as some people change hairdressers." I found this a rather sexist comment. But in that this was meant to characterize Ms. E.C. as a patient known to go from doctor to doctor because of her displeasure with their recommendations, (thus costing her insurance company and the health care system loads of money), it was accurate.

Furthermore, it would later be reported that she felt her problems centered around an "allergy" to thyroid medication. However, my medical evaluation revealed that she had inappropriately been taking dangerous doses of thyroid hormone in order to treat her "condition." Without going into detail, suffice it to say that I spent an extraordinary amount of time explaining to Ms. E.C. that excessive thyroid treatment could result in potentially fatal organ failure.

I did not feel she was suffering from a drug deficiency, or a drug allergy.

Being a strong advocate in lifestyle changes and dietary

changes to treat medical disease, as well as a strong advocate of preventive medical care, I recommended appropriate thyroid dosing and discussed in detail a specific dietary, exercise, and lifestyle program for weight reduction, disease risk reduction, and improved general health.

In my evaluation, I sensed that she was displeased that I had not recommended more thyroid testing, and was clearly displeased that I recommended that she assume more personal responsibility for her medical health. (If one were to see and meet Ms. E.C. in person, it would not be difficult to ascertain what I might have recommended that she found so offensive). Nevertheless, I took the time to fully explain my rationale, and the basis for my recommendations.

After this difficult and prolonged visit, Ms. E.C. was billed a consult fee of $200. This was the highest level of consult fee I had charged in my previous practice, and I had not yet charged this amount of outpatient consult fee in my current practice. This unusual case included a fee for an extensive medical evaluation (history and physical exam), complete review of health problems and health risks, medical and lifestyle recommendations, review of laboratory, and a dictated report to her referring doctor.

This fee also included overhead costs such as office space and equipment, highly-trained office staff (with benefits), administration costs of loading the patient information into the office computer, subsequent filing of insurance claims, taxes, and other costs involved in running any small business.

Despite what I felt was a reasonable charge for my services, Ms. E.C. sent a letter of complaint to the Jefferson County Medical Society (JCMS). This was, and continues to be, the only letter of complaint about any aspect of my practice of medicine. (Conversely, I have received many letters of recognition for my participation in charitable causes of the JCMS). Considering the amount of time spent with her, considering the hundreds of dollars of health care dollars saved because I declined to order unnecessary thyroid scans, X-rays, etc., I felt my charges justified. And I stated as such in a response letter to the JCMS.

And to be clear, the patient was informed of the potential range of initial consultant fees before the appointment was made. If, by chance she forgot, or was unclear as to the potential range of charges, this information was readily available at anytime. The point being, Ms. E.C. was not a helpless victim of the healthcare system. Rather, she was an empowered consumer who had a choice to see me, a subspecialist for the quoted price, or go elsewhere for a lesser fee. Her freedom to choose her doctor based on potential charges is a freedom granted to all citizens in the free enterprise system.

This is known as capitalism.

Hence, the JCMS did not feel that further action was warranted. Ms. E.C. did not feel that appeal through the JCMS was warranted. Ms. E.C. did not feel that legal action was warranted.

Nevertheless, although I had no obligation to do so, I subsequently refunded $103 of the $200 charge in 1992. Ms. E.C. documented her acceptance of this refund in her letter dated August 5, 1992, closing and resolving the matter - or so it seemed.

GOTCHA

From 1992 until 1994, many changes had taken place.

Los Angeles had race riots due to the Rodney King beating verdict.

Ross Perot energized a segment of the electorate to almost third party status.

Dan Quayle criticized Murphy Brown, a fictional TV character.

George Bush lost an election.

Bill Clinton won an election.

Talk radio flourished.

And a proposed government-run health care system failed to gain public support, and died.

During this same period, I had left my previous practice and had set up my own medical practice from scratch. I established my own billing procedure, my own accounting system, and my own policy with regard to contracts with insurance companies. In essence, I took the same risks, and made the similar efforts that many other entrepreneurs take every day.

I worked countless hours towards starting my own small business.

A short time later, I was joined by another Endocrinologist. Because of her impeccable academic background and caring relationship with her patients, I felt she and I had a bright future together, and I looked forward towards achieving our goal to provide the best care for patients.

All the while, massive changes in medicine were occurring due to the influx of managed care. But despite the declining reimbursements from insurers, I was optimistic and excited about my new practice and my new partner. And I was particularly excited about my research that I hoped would help my medical colleagues improve, and perhaps save the lives of their patients.

But as I was living the American Dream, the press was soon to transform my life into an American Nightmare.

Gotcha.

On Thursday May 26, 1994, at 11 AM, I was in the midst of writing a manuscript of the results of my research on the use of diabetes pills in hemodialysis patients. I suddenly received an emergency message on my pager asking me to call the office. I was informed that a reporter from the Gannett Courier-Journal (the only state-wide newspaper in Kentucky) had called to notify me that I was the subject of a investigative report of overcharging by doctors. I had one day to return his call, otherwise the story was to run "as is" (i.e. without my input).

"Gotcha."

I immediately called the Gannett reporter back, who then stated that he was writing a story about health care costs. His premise was how I, as a *medical specialist,* overcharged patients compared to generalists who performed the same level of service.

At first, I suggested that he was in error as I had no recollection of this patient. But after at least 20 frantic phone calls, I determined that I did see Ms. E.C. over two years prior. However, I challenged his "specialist vs. generalist" premise. Ms. E.C. had failed to inform the Gannett reporter that her previous doctor was a specialist in Internal Medicine - not a generalist. I found it disturbing that after three months of research, he had not as yet confirmed the very basis of his story.

He then stated that his premise was how I, as a representative of a *medical specialty group,* overcharged patients.

I explained that this event had occurred while I was an employee at another practice, and that I had left this practice over a year before. I now was a partner in my own medical practice.

He then stated that his premise was how I, as a *single doctor,* overcharged patients.

(At this point, I was becoming dizzy trying to keep up with the ever-changing premise).

I explained that Ms. E.C.'s billing complaint was an

isolated event that occurred due to extraordinary circumstances. Also, although I had no obligation to do so, I
voluntarily refunded this patient over 1/2 of my consult fee
in 1992. (Although Ms. E..C. had full recollection of the
amount of medical charges, I found it revealing that she had
selectively forgotten the refund). Furthermore, the 1992
charges in my previous practice had nothing to do with 1994
charges in my current practice. And finally, due to the
massive influx of managed care, the reimbursement rate
from insurers to doctors in 1992 had little semblance to the
reimbursement rate in 1994.

He then stated that his premise was how I charged Ms. E.C.
$200 for the same level of medical service that her previous
doctor had only charged $35.

To this day, I still don't know where he dreamed up this
fantasy. I explained to the Gannett reporter that this was
blatantly incorrect. Letters and billing statements clearly
documented that, including the refund, I was paid $97 for a
45 - 60 minute complex consult fee, and subsequent 3 page
dictated medical evaluation report to her referring doctor.
Her previous doctor charged $75 for a 10 - 15 minute quick
office visit.

This was an obvious, and blatant misstatement of fact. Did
he really think reasonable people would believe that the
previous doctor had only charged $35 for a complete
medical evaluation? How many highly trained medical
specialists agree to perform a 45 - 60 minute initial medical
history and physical examination, a review of organ
systems, a review of past and present medical history, a

discussion of preventive medical care, an explanation of the pathophysiology of the disease state, a detailed outline of the appropriate treatment for the disease state, a review of preventive medical care, and a dictated letter - all for $35?

$35?

How many plumbers only charge $35 for an initial visit?

I recently had my lawnmower serviced at Sears. The bill stated that the repairman (who may, or may not have had a high school education) had worked for 20 minutes to clean the carburetor. The charge was $46.

But yet the Gannett reporter hoped to enhance his premise by dreaming up a fictitious $35 charge. The creation of this fantasy was an act of a desperate reporter. And I could certainly understand his despair. Despite repeated attempts to create a story, every turn was leading to a dead end. And, at least with regard to my involvement, the story he had promised his editors for three months was a non-story because he had based his ever changing premise on misleading statements by the accuser - without ever considering getting the facts from the accused until the last minute.

Nevertheless, the Gannett editors had given him a deadline to provide them a story, and he was obliged to create them one.

DENIAL

"This can't be happening to me," I thought.

Not only was I being wrongfully and unfairly accused, but I was largely held defenseless due to concerns of patient confidentiality. Without Ms. E.C.'s permission, I could not discuss her case.

But even though this Thursday had been one of the worst days of my life, the rest of the week was to prove to be even worse. The following morning started upon rising at 5:45 AM to meet my research patients at the metabolic center for which I am Medical Director. The remainder of the morning and afternoon was reserved for my downtown private practice patients. Afterward, I had hospital rounds. In the midst of my hectic schedule of doing those things that doctors do, the Gannett reporter had rushed to meet with Ms. E.C. that same morning, and urgently faxed me a written statement, granting me permission to release any and all aspects of her case with the press. In Ms. E.C.'s letter of May 27, 1994, she stated,

> "Dr. Bays:
>
> "You have my permission to discuss my medical condition with [the press], and to

> release documents, records and/or letters
> concerning your treatment of me in 1992 to
> [the press]. This would include any records
> or information relating to billing or to the
> basis for that billing, (but would not be
> limited to that)."

But since I had little to no recollection of this patient, this was of marginal help. I vented my frustration to the Gannett reporter that afternoon. I expressed concern that he had been writing this story for three months, had a personal interview with the accuser three weeks prior, and had now threatened me with only one day to respond to an isolated 2 year old billing complaint. It was after this protest that the Gannett reporter agreed to meet with me - the accused - only hours before his stated deadline.

Hence, in addition to the pressure of the medical management of complicated research patients, office patients, and hospital patients, I now had the pressure of requesting, locating, and reviewing the medical and billing details of a two year old case involving a forgotten patient seen while as an employee at another medical practice. Furthermore, I had to hastily prepare a response that could forever affect my life. I had no opportunity for counsel. I had no opportunity to reflect and respond.

"Gotcha."

And I could not understand why this story was so pressing - other than perhaps the Gannett reporter got caught behind a deadline. Was it because he didn't have the courage to tell his editors that after three months of research, he

49

discovered only hours before his deadline that he had no story?

On that Friday meeting with the bearded Pat Howington (the Gannett "investigative" reporter), I emphasized that the $200 charge was the highest amount I had charged any patient. I obtained and fully disclosed documentation that I had yet to charge such an office consult fee in my current practice. Also during this meeting, I objected to having one day opportunity to respond to a two year old isolated billing complaint.

"This can't be happening to me."

After all my commitment to academia, and charitable causes, I could not believe that the importance of this one disgruntled patient would warrant damage to a lifelong reputation. Nevertheless, I remained fully cooperative, and did not hesitate to enter into a dialogue with the Gannett Courier-Journal. I offered full and total disclosure of all personal and financial files. It was my feeling that previous condemnations of doctors by the Gannett Courier-Journal were probably because doctors were too arrogant to take the time and to make the effort to respond.

After all, I felt that journalists were basically good, decent, hard working people trying to do a job that had constitutional purpose and merit. Furthermore, since I had faith that reporters and editors had an uncompromising dedication to truth, and an unyielding respect and compassion for the reputation of the very citizens they had a constitutional obligation to protect, I felt my willingness to cooperate would ensure accuracy and fairness.

Because it is the dedication to protecting individual liberties through reporting the truth that defines journalism as a profession.

The following Saturday, for reasons unclear, no story had yet been published. I then began to fax letters on a daily basis to Gannett to guarantee that the reporter was provided the facts. It was my thinking that if I could document that the Gannett reporter knew the truth before the story was published, he would be ethically bound to report the truth. And if he reported the truth, then my involvement in this story would be noncontributory and negligible.

By the following Tuesday, the story had still not yet been published. Later that day, I had another phone conversation with the Gannett reporter who stated that he still intended to report that I had charged Ms. E.C. $200 for the same level of office service provided by her previous doctor for $35. Because this was the central issue with regard to my involvement, I was very disturbed by this misstatement of fact. I referred the Gannett reporter to Ms. E.C.'s letter regarding the relative charges and to actual billing statements. And I even sent several letters confirming this crucial issue.

In a 5/29/94 letter, I stated,

> "Nevertheless, my $97 consult charge ($200 - $103) in 1992 was still more than that charged by one of her (many) previous doctors. I believe her [previous doctor] was a specialist in Internal Medicine charged her

$75 in 1991. Is their documentation that her [previous doctor] did as complex a evaluation as I?"

In a 5/31/94 letter, I stated,

"I fear that your article will state or imply that my $97 office consultation represented a higher fee for no more effort than Ms. E.C.'s previous doctor who charged $75 for a "10 - 15 minute" initial visit for a "routine thyroid evaluation" and medication refill in 1991. This allegation is false. Many Internal Medicine Specialists do allow for a 10 minute initial office visit for such level of care. However, it was the office policy of [my previous practice], and it remains the office policy of my current office that no patients are seen for less than 30 minutes, and are typically seen for 45 to 60 minutes. I have documentation that my evaluation included history, physical exam, review of systems, review of preventative medicine issues, social history, family history, discussion of her thyroid status, and extensive discussion of what I believed to be the main source of her medical complaints - an unwillingness to accept medical advice concerning life style changes that would improve her current and future health. A review of her previous doctor's records will document that she did not perform as complete and complex evaluation as I. Also she did not further review the clinical findings and laboratory findings afterward that were outlined in a prepared 2 1/2 page manuscript to the referring doctor."

And to document that the Gannett reporter had received the facts, the 5/31/95 letter began with,

> "This is the final letter that I am faxing (and will subsequently mail) concerning the Courier's coverage of 2/92 allegations of overcharging by Ms. E.C. against me. I hope you have carefully read and considered the facts of the three previous letters faxed to you on 5/27, 5/28, and 5/29. If these are somehow not available to you during any point in the preparation of your story, if you no longer have copies of these letters, or if you have any questions or doubts as to their accuracy, meaning or substance, please feel free to call me immediately."

Afterwards, the Gannett reporter sent me a fax stating,

> "I got the letter you faxed to me this morning."

Despite all the documentation, the Gannett reporter insisted that he was going to report the $200/$35 fee discrepancy. In disbelief, I protested. Since it is the dedication to protecting individual liberties through reporting the truth that defines journalism as a profession, why would he, as a journalist, not report the truth?

It was his explanation of the need to report this misstatement in a phone conversation that prompted this book.

THE PERSPECTIVE

The Gannett reporter informed me that I was being narrow-minded in my concerns and objections to this story. He stated that the specific factual aspects of this case were not nearly as important as the "perspective" of the story.

I am not kidding.

Unbelievable.

I replied that I didn't want to be a perspective - especially when it was my name that would be on the pages. I told him that rather than achieving his "perspective," I would just as soon he be accurate.

But it was now clear that the Gannett reporter was not as interested in reporting the facts as much as he was interested in reporting that I was a greedy doctor. And as the hours and days went by, I was becoming increasingly paranoid about the Gannett reporter's assertion that perspective mattered more than accuracy. What other misstatement of facts was he was going to report? And on what page would this story be published? Would it be buried on a back page, hard to find section, or, as I feared most, perhaps on the front page of the City/Metro section (B1)?

As a result of my increasing concerns, I requested a meeting with the Gannett reporter and his editor - Gideon Gill. Again, it was my thinking that if I documented that the Gannett reporter knew the truth before the story was published, he would be ethically bound to print the truth. And if he reported the truth, no story existed and the story would die.

At the very beginning of this face-to-face, tape-recorded meeting of 6/2/94, the Gannett editor gave me his assurance that before he allowed the Gannett reporter to print any article, it would be accurate, as well as fair to me, and fair to doctors.

I was reassured and thankful.

I again pleaded that the Gannett reporter print the truth with regard to the $200 office charges of my 45 - 60 minute medical evaluation compared to Ms. E.C.'s previous doctor's $75 office charge for 10 - 15 minute evaluation. This time, the Gannett reporter agreed to print the truth.

I was reassured and thankful.

Finally, the Gannett reporter initiated a conversation concerning doctor's pay. In a letter of 5/28/94, I stated,

> "It is also telling that despite 5 years of practice, despite seeing 15 - 20 of among the most complicated patients a day, despite being on call 24 hours a day except for 2 days every other weekend, my income through the practice (minus payments

towards my share of the Corporate loan which I think is fair overhead consideration for any business) netted for the past year at $37,778. I own no stocks. I have no retirement plan in my current practice. I would be willing to fully disclose my financial records on this matter to prove this figure accurate."

The Gannett reporter inquired as to why I wanted my income published. I replied that the Gannett Courier-Journal had demonstrated in the past a pathologic and bizarre obsession towards publishing the incomes of citizens they felt deserved class condemnation. Therefore, since my income was probably not high enough to elicit the petty jealously so desperately sought by Gannett, I thought it relevant to report my real-life income.

The Gannett reporter then spent some time convincing me that this article had nothing to do with doctor's pay. (Meanwhile, his editor, was sitting next to him as the tape recorder ran.) After some discussion, I reluctantly agreed that if the article was not to address doctor's pay, my income would not be relevant.

And I was reassured and thankful.

THE STORY

On June 4, 1994, the article was published.

It was beyond my worst fears.

No, the article was not reported on a back page, hard-to-find section of the paper.

No, it was not even reported on the front page of the City/Metro section (B1).

Instead, the Gannett editors felt that my conduct was so monstrous as to warrant a front page, lead headline story of the day. (See Appendix)

Page A1.

"Gotcha."

Note that despite all conversations, letters, faxes, face-to-face meetings, and promises, the Gannett reporter followed through on his promise to misstate the facts.

Note that despite giving his word that my pay as a doctor had nothing to do with the story, he included a large chart listing "Doctor's Pay" indicating my income as an Endocrinologist was over $100,000. He chose not to report my true income of $37,778.

The Courier – Journal

Woman changes doctors, almost triples her bill

By PATRICK HOWINGTON
Staff Writer

E.C. has gotten the...,

. . .

The endocrinologist she went to that year charged her $200 for the office visit, almost six times the $35 charge that an internist had charged her the year before. . .

Picture of German Soldiers

A German soldier on leave cleaned the graves . . .

SECOND STORY

Directly to the right of the front page, lead story of the day was a story about the 50th anniversary of D-Day. On June 6, 1994, directed by General Dwight D. Eisenhower, the Allied troops attacked the beaches of Normandy. Hitler was taken by surprise and the Allies gained a foot-hold in the European theater, with the eventual fall of Nazi Germany. The story, "War and Peace," described how, on the 50th anniversary of this historic event, the Germans remembered the 78,000 Germans buried in Norman graves, and how the world reacted to Germany 50 years later.

FRONT PAGE, LEAD HEADLINE STORY OF THE DAY

The lead story "Woman changes doctors, almost triples her bill" made no specific allegations of wrongdoing, illegal acts, or unethical behavior. It simply reported significantly fabricated facts regarding an isolated billing dispute that was resolved with a refund over 2 years prior, that occurred while the doctor was an employee at another practice, and that was brought forth by a disgruntled woman who "changed doctors as often as some people change hairdressers." The article's intent was to portray doctors as greedy bastards.

QUESTIONS

This doctor had done nothing illegal. His only "crime" was being a doctor. The reporter initially threatened a one business day opportunity for the doctor to respond. Was this a violation of The Fifth Amendment Miranda right to counsel before responding? And considering the deception in the research of this story, was this a violation of the Fifth Amendment right that "no person shall be held to answer for a ... crime...without due process of law?"

And why is an isolated billing dispute of more journalistic merit, and a greater atrocity than issues surrounding the D-Day invasion of World War II, and the subsequent fall of a Nazi regime?

Note that despite that I had nothing to do with the fees of my previous practice, it was my name that was mentioned 11 times.

And note that the Gannett Courier-Journal editors made a conscious, painstaking journalistic decision that my actions were so heinous as to warrant public condemnation through a significantly fabricated, front page, lead headline story of the day.

They determined that an isolated two year old billing complaint that took place while I was an employee at another practice, that was resolved with a refund, and that originated from a woman who had been known to "change doctors as often as other people change hairdressers" warranted front page national priority over:

> "2 Fugitive murderers are found in New York" (Page A2)
>
> "Explosion kills three men in San Francisco" (Page A4)
>
> "Clinton honors WWII soldiers who freed Italy" (Page A6)
>
> "Vandals ravage Caney school as lawsuit over closing languishes" (Page A10)
>
> "State asks judge to rule on whether Medicaid must pay for certain abortions" (Page A13)
>
> "Religious right makes state-by-state gains in controlling the GOP" (Page A13)
>
> "A_____ G_____, 25, address unavailable. Charged with second degree burglary. Pleaded

guilty to amended charge of first-degree criminal trespass. Placed on probation for two years. Charges of third-degree criminal trespass, volatile substance abuse, resisting arrest, disorderly conduct and theft by unlawful taking dismissed." (Page A13)

This isolated billing complaint was not the death of a President. It was not an announcement of war. It was not a natural disaster. Nor was it a terrorist bombing of a Trade Center or a Midwestern city. But yet this significantly fabricated, isolated billing complaint somehow warranted the front page, lead headline story of the day.

ANGER

Printed words on a page cannot express the emotions I felt, and the hardship to my family, when this article appeared on page A1. I had lived and worked in many different areas across the state of Kentucky. I had always tried to conduct myself in an ethical and professional manner. And being among the financially poorest members of my medical school class, I had hoped to set an example of how anyone from any background can succeed in the ''big city.'' (Louisville). But because of this article, I was being portrayed as some type of villain. People I would never meet again would forever think me a criminal.

Even today, it is difficult to adequately describe my frustration. However, the following excerpts from some of my letters provide some insight:

> ''And please consider, how will this story affect the confidence of my medical patients? How will this affect the confidence of my study patients, many who are on experimental medications? How will this affect the referral of patients who might have benefitted from my unique area of expertise? How will this affect my interactions with friends? How will this affect my wife's interactions with friends?

How will this affect my in-laws? How will this affect my father and brothers? How will this affect my mother? These may seem irrelevant and contrived concerns to you compared to your need to print your story by Monday. But these people constitute my life, and are a very real concern to me."

(Letter to Gannett reporter May 26th, 1994 - before the article)

....

"The slant of this story is particularly painful to me as I have spent far more time as a physician trying to build a reputation, than trying to build a fortune. Unfortunately, after this story, I will have lost much of my reputation. Had I been trying to build a fortune, I at least could have kept the money. All I ask is that you remember that Ms. E.C. has registered an unprovoked, isolated complaint against me (one of her many doctors), even after I believe I fairly resolved this issue 2 years ago."

(Letter to Gannett reporter 5/28/94 - before the article)

....

"You may wonder why I have been so apprehensive about the story regarding allegations of Ms. E.C.. Understand, I do not fear the truth. I have all confidence that you will be factual. However, I do fear the incomplete truth."

(Letter to Gannett reporter 5/31/94 - before the article)

Mr. Howington, regardless of the final form of your story, my family and I have already been wrongfully punished. And after the story, the medical profession will be punished as well. But as you write, I hope you will remember that I have allowed a level of disclosure of my personal and financial life that must be unprecedented. I am among the most private persons I know. Words cannot describe how painful it is to me to feel required to expose my life to strangers. But as much as I value my privacy, I value my reputation more. Ask yourself, how many other physicians would have responded in this open a manner. And also ask yourself, if you were wrongfully accused about an event that took place over 2 years ago, and if the decision to print these accusations in a state-wide newspaper was made long before your were asked to respond, would you be so forthcoming with your personal affairs?

(Letter to Gannett reporter 5/31/94 - before the article)

"My Mother, who is paralyzed in the legs due to a damaged cervical disc, was first presented with this article, during a rehabilitation out-patient visit, when the nurses...showed her the article about how her son was a criminal. My colleagues who know me are sympathetic to my position and are outraged at the Courier-Journal. My colleagues who don't know me are uncertain. My practice has suffered. My family and practice have been wrongfully harmed.''

(Manuscript given to Lead Editor, and Vice President of the Gannett Courier-Journal 6/30/94 - after the article)

....

I had been tried and convicted during trial by the press. And as the convicted criminal, what credible response could I give to my family?

"Don't believe 'em Ma. I didn't do it Ma"

"I was framed.''

Anger.

First of all, I was angry that I had been given only one day to initially respond to a complaint from a bitter, disgruntled woman who by the reporter's own admission "changed doctors as often as other people change hairdressers.'' I should have been granted more time to review the case before responding. And had I been given time to seek counsel first, perhaps I would have been advised to not speak to the reporter at all.

Secondly, I was angry that an article about an isolated billing complaint, that took place while an employee at another practice, and that was resolved with a refund two years prior, somehow warranted a front page, lead headline story of the day, and somehow warranted printing my name 11 times.

But most of all I was angry that the Gannett reporter deliberately misstated the facts of the story so as to create his "perspective." Furthermore, in the most contemptible of acts, he included a chart of "Doctor's Pay" after he had given me his word in a face-to-face, tape-recorded meeting in front of his editor that this article had nothing to do with doctor's pay. And although it may not be politically correct, please note the following definition:

> Lie: v.,
>
> 1. (a) to make a statement that one knows is false, esp. with intent to deceive (b) to make such statements habitually
>
> 2. (a) to give a false impression

Using this definition, the Gannett reporter had lied to me. And worst of all, the Gannett reporter had lied to the reader.

Subsequently, I requested an opportunity to defend myself in a "letter to the editor."

My request was ignored.

THE MEETING

I then requested a face-to-face meeting with David Hawpe - the bearded lead editor and Vice President of the Gannett Courier-Journal. When I entered his office, he was noticeably agitated and angry. He had a stack of papers prepared and was clearly ready to refute any arguments I brought forth. Nevertheless, I kept my cool and methodically provided page after page of detailed documentation of the inaccurate and unprofessional reporting of the Gannett reporter. I also provided documentation of the profound impact this story had on my family, and on my income as depicted by the devastating drop in the scheduling of patients.

By sticking with the documented facts, point after point went by without any refutation. However, we did have several areas of disagreement.

First, he stated that he would not print my "letter to the editor" without an op-ed response that "would only prolong the matter and make things worse for you." Given that Gannett had proven itself capable and willing to publish just about anything, I took this threat very seriously. Nevertheless, I was disappointed in his position.

I felt I deserved a right to defend my reputation.

And at least my "letter to the editor" was the truth.

He did however, agree to publish my wife's letter.

Dr. Bays' Achievement

In reference to the Courier-Journal's June 4 article about my husband, Dr. Harold Bays, the C-J chose the wrong physician if it was trying to expose him as a materialistic physician (as The C-J has a tendency to do when writing about health care). My husband leaves for the office in the mornings in his "stylish" 1987 Pontiac Grand Am, purchased used from Budget Rent-A-Car. Also, he is not exactly obsessed with fashion. Up until a few weeks ago, he only owned three pairs of shoes (this included one pair of athletic shoes and two pairs of re-soled loafers).

Furthermore, my husband volunteers and gives medical attention to the men staying at the Healing Place, a shelter for homeless men. Also, he volunteers his time to participate in benefits, sponsored by the American Diabetes Association, to raise funds for diabetes research. Often these events require him to drive, to and from Louisville, for two to three hours (after a day of seeing patients at the office and the hospital), and he usually arrives home after midnight.

Finally, I wonder why Patrick Howington

failed to mention any of my husband's credentials. My husband achieved some of the top scores on the National Board examinations in Internal Medicine, as well as in Endocrinology and Metabolism. Also, he has published several medical research articles worldwide. I know, firsthand, the time and effort that were put into these achievements.

After reading the above, I hope you can understand that, for me, the article was not about health care and the need for reform. We all agree reform is needed. However, the facts surrounding this isolated case, resolved in 1992, shed no light into the problem or the solutions surrounding health care reform in 1994. Wake up, 1992 was two years ago!

D. Bays

Secondly, the Lead Editor and Vice President surprisingly agreed with the Gannett reporter's argument that the perspective of a story mattered more than the specific facts of a story. I again found this an unfortunate position.

Thirdly, he indicated a lack of understanding as to why I was so upset. He could not fathom how a front page, lead headline condemnation article implying that I overcharge patients warranted such concern. In fact, he offered to take me out to a "steak dinner" if this story proved to harm my practice.

I then showed him my office schedule proving that before the story, I had a thriving practice booked up for three weeks in advance. After the story, my scheduled patients dropped to the point that I had to cancel entire days in the office. Without missing a beat, he then revised his promise with an offer to take me out to a steak dinner if this story proved to harm my practice in a year.

Although much has been said about the out-of-touch, elite press, one does have to admire this degree of flexibility.

The final point of contention was a very telling moment concerning the Gannett reporter's initial one day threat. After I objected to this form of journalism, this lead editor and Vice President of a major Gannett newspaper stated,

"We don't do that."

He sternly stated that the "gotcha" investigative mentality is not tolerated at the Gannett Courier-Journal. Furthermore, he showed me a computer print out provided to him by the Gannett reporter "documenting" that I had personally been notified about this story three weeks before publication.

There ensued a sudden, telling moment that will forever be etched upon my mind.

Although it may not be politically correct, I think it would be appropriate to once again review the following definition:

Lie: v.,

1. (a) to make a statement that one knows is false, esp. with intent to deceive (b) to make such statements habitually

2. (a) to give a false impression

A considerable bit of silence went by after his statement. It was clear that the Gannett reporter had not only lied to me about the story's content regarding doctor's pay, not only lied to the reader about my relative office charges, but now had flat-out lied to his editor as to when I was first notified of the story.

After a few deep breaths, I calmly provided documentation proving this to be untrue. I convincingly demonstrated that I had not been notified three weeks before the story. I clearly demonstrated that the Gannett reporter had engaged in "gotcha" journalism. And I provided proof that the Gannett reporter had now mislead his own editor as to when I was first notified of the story.

And in the end, even the lead editor and Vice President had to admit,

> "I believe you were not notified of this article
> sooner."

As the meeting progressed, I sensed that this lead editor had understood, and appreciated, the wrong that had been committed.

After all, the press was basically composed of decent, hard-working people with the highest level of integrity. And although from time to time, I may have disagreed with the political editorials, when it came to reporting the news, I had faith that editors had an uncompromising dedication to truth, and an unyielding respect and compassion for the reputation of the very citizens they had a constitutional obligation to protect.

Believing as such, I felt that this lead editor and I had truly connected. Although he had started out the meeting in anger, I could not help but feel that he now understood how I had been wronged, and would make things right. In fact, near the end of the meeting, he sympathetically asked:

"What can we do?"

First and foremost, I requested that any future articles against doctors be truthful and fair. I also requested that Gannett report some of my positive contributions to the community to help me regain some of my reputation wrongfully lost.

I was impressed with his concern. Not only did he seem to listen, but this lead editor and Vice President of a major Gannett newspaper took notes and assured me that he would have someone inquire about my medical research, and my physician volunteer work for the homeless.

As I was about to leave on the elevator, he gave me his word that he would take personal responsibility for future stories on physicians, and guaranteed they would be accurate and fair. Finally, he requested that if I ever thought that the Gannett Courier-Journal was unfair to the medical profession, I was to personally let him know.

And although it was not stated or implied in any way, I had every confidence that he, having the awesome responsibility as a lead editor of the free press, would surely put an ethical leash on the Gannett reporter.

But this was to prove to be yet another fantasy.

The extraordinary events that subsequently occurred were so surrealistic, that even today it seemed more fiction than reality. It was inconceivable to me that the Gannett reporter would again be allowed to continue his reckless brand of inaccurate journalism, causing unwarranted and preventable harm to more innocent citizens simply because they made the unfortunate career choice to be doctors in the state of Kentucky.

But the Gannett reporter *was* given such a forum - again. He would soon be rewarded with another front page, lead headline story of the day, wherein he would inaccurately and wrongfully harm the reputations of doctors.

The Courier – Journal

Medicaid has first million-dollar doctor

EIGHT TOP

$500,000

FROM STATE

By PATRICK HOWINGTON
and JOSEPH GERTH

Staff Writers

Black Civil War soldiers honored

Picture of Black Civil War Soldiers

SECOND STORY

Directly below the front page, lead headline story of the day was a picture of "Black Civil War Soldiers." From 1861-65, the United States underwent one of the bloodiest civil wars in history with over a half a million deaths, countless disfiguring injuries, and unfathomable misery. Many of the issues surrounding this war (often pitting brother against brother) continue to have ramifications today. One of the moral dimensions of the war centered around the Emancipation Proclamation which ended the practice of using black human beings as slaves. Afterwards, the "United States Colored Troops" came into being. This article described the African American Civil War Memorial, the work of Louisville sculptor Ed Hamilton, as the first memorial recognizing the 178,000 black soldiers who fought in the Civil War.

FRONT PAGE, LEAD HEADLINE STORY OF THE DAY

The lead story "Medicaid has first million dollar doctor - Eight Top $500,000 From State" made no specific allegations of wrongdoing, illegal acts, or unethical behavior. It simply listed the incomes of specific doctors with the intent to portray doctors as greedy bastards. Subsequently, the incomes listed were found to be blatantly misleading. But the correction was buried in the body text of a subsequent issue of the newspaper. The reporter has yet to apologize.

QUESTIONS

The specific doctors whose names were listed were never given the opportunity to respond before they were "convicted" in the press. Was this a violation of The Sixth Amendment of the Constitution that grants the right to "be informed of the nature and cause of the accusation?"

Why is the misleading report of income of doctors of more journalistic merit than honoring 178,000 black soldiers who fought in the Civil War?

YET MORE ANGER

In a continuing attack of class warfare, the next target of the Gannett reporter was on physicians who cared for the poor. In this next front page, lead headline "investigative report," he listed the payments that some Kentucky doctors had received from Medicaid. On the chart were the specific dollar amounts supposedly paid by Medicaid to specific doctors. The doctors' names were included.

The article was intended to portray doctors as greedy bastards - again.

But, not unexpectedly, it was later determined that many of these payments were yet another fabrication of an irresponsible Gannett reporter who had a pathologic, and bizarre obsession with doctors' income. In reality, the money listed as going to doctors were actually charges billed to the state in the name of doctors who worked in clinics that provided care for the poor. The actual payments did not go directly to the doctors at all, but rather went to the clinics they served. The doctors only received a small percentage of the amounts listed.

The Gannett reporter had just publicly ridiculed doctors who cared for the poor.

Why did this happen - again?

Why did the Gannett reporter fail to seek reasonable input from the very citizens he was about to condemn? This was not a breaking story. There was no rush. How difficult could it have been to pick up the telephone and confirm the facts before reporting another fantasy? His error was easily avoidable.

But instead, accuracy took a second priority over perspective, and he again listed a chart of doctors' incomes that was grossly misleading.

Why?

Because the Gannett reporter had the perspective that doctors rightly deserved repeated public humiliation and condemnation - simply because they were doctors. And he was journalistically driven to impart this perspective to the public - at all costs. No level of deceit was too great, and no misstatement was too blatant to stand in the way of the Gannett reporter's perspective. If it had not been clear before, this second injustice was confirmation that the Gannett reporter was a dangerous and calloused human being.

As a result of this atrocity, the Gannett Courier-Journal granted doctors a reprieve. The Gannett reporter was required to print a correction regarding the inaccuracies of stated incomes of doctors. But, while as his "gotcha" article was the front page (A1), lead headline story of the day, the correction was buried in section B.

This was an outrage. And it was revealing that this Gannett reporter's malicious and unwarranted attacks were finally wearing thin, even among his colleagues. In an almost unprecedented act, the ombudsman, as well as other Gannett reporter colleagues openly published their disagreement with this reporter's inaccurate and mean-spirited attack on doctors.

This makes the important point. Although bad reporters and editors exist, it should be stated that most of those who work in the press are probably decent, hard-working persons with the highest level of integrity. And it is their dedication to protecting individual liberties through reporting the truth that defines journalism as a profession.

Their open support for the wrongfully accused was a honorable and brave act. It was reassuring that some in the press felt compelled to make some effort to correct this repeated injustice against innocent citizens by an irresponsible reporter.

Meanwhile, the Gannett reporter, blamed it all on a "misunderstanding."

But while his latest victims were granted apologies and corrections, I had yet to receive similar consideration, despite experiencing a similar injustice. Furthermore, the misstatements against me were anything but a "misunderstanding." Unbelievably, the wrongful damage to my family and reputation by the Gannett Courier-Journal elicited quite a different response.

After my face-to-face meeting with the lead editor, the lead editor and Vice President gave me his word that Gannett would inquire as to my medical research efforts, as well as my volunteer efforts with the homeless.

No such inquiries ever occurred. His word would prove as reliable as his reporter's "perspective."

After the article, I sent letters to the Gannett reporter responsible for this story, to other reporters, to the editor of the opinion pages, to the associate editor, and to the managing editor.

I sent a lot of letters.

But I received nothing in return. I received no correspondence, no phone call, nor any response at all. Finally, out of desperation, and out of an attempt to avoid litigation and going through attorneys, I contacted the ombudsman.

The position of ombudsman had been established by the Courier-Journal before the buy-out by Gannett. And it was the purpose of the ombudsman to act as liaison between the Courier-Journal and those citizens who were treated unfairly in newspaper reports. In theory, if a citizen felt he/she had been wronged, the ombudsman would serve as something as an arbitrator, presumably with an unbiased desire to help foster the highest ethical conduct at the Courier-Journal.

But after my appeal to the ombudsman, I did not receive arbitration. I received no return explanatory phone call or letter after his inquiries. Instead, my objections to wrongful acts of the press were sent directly to the Gannett Corporate attorney who proceeded to send a threatening letter.

THE THREAT

In his letter, the Gannett attorney stated that although inaccuracies clearly existed, these were "minor," and thus did not warrant further consideration. He advised that I drop the matter.

I appreciated that the Gannett Corporate attorney took the time to give me advice. But I think most folks would agree that intentional misstatements (can I use the word "lie" again?) and deliberate mean-spirited attacks on the reputations of innocent citizens were anything but minor.

But the Corporate Gannett attorney was not finished. He also made it clear that Gannett would not hesitate to use the constitutional privilege of "freedom of the press" as a powerful weapon. He made it clear that Gannett would publicly punish me if I chose to pursue litigation in order to recover damages for loss of reputation and loss of income as the direct result of intentional, and malicious wrongdoings of an irresponsible Gannett reporter.

He threatened that, if I chose to seek justice through litigation, Gannett would surely publish those parts of the story that I found "distasteful."

But the only aspects of the story I found "distasteful" were the intentional misstatement of fact. If the truth had been published, this story would not have been distasteful.

However, I did find it distasteful that, despite acts of malice to harm me simply because I am a doctor, the Gannett reporter was not sanctioned and harnessed. In fact, he was rewarded with yet another opportunity to engage in class warfare with another misleading, inaccurate and malicious front page, lead headline article against doctors. I found it distasteful that even his own colleagues finally felt compelled to condemn this unprofessional and unwarranted reporting.

And I found it distasteful that I had not yet received a single letter or phone call giving a simple apology for the wrongful harm to my family and reputation as the result of inaccurate reporting (in which my name was listed 11 times) about an isolated billing complaint that occurred two years prior, while I was an employee at another practice.

These things I found distasteful.

And who knows how much of the rest of the article was also fantasy. Who knows how much of the rest of the article was simply fabricated to create his "perspective."

Admittedly, even if this article had been printed factually, I would have still felt it ridiculous that such a story merited a front page, lead headline article. But my main concern was the issue of accuracy and fairness. As silly as the headline was in its original form,

"WOMAN CHANGES DOCTOR,
ALMOST TRIPLES HER BILL"

if the truth had been reported, the front page, lead headline
would have been,

"WOMAN GETS THREE TIMES THE
CARE, THREE TIMES THE CHARGE,
THEN GETS REFUND"

This would have been equally silly. But at least with regard
to my involvement, it would have been the truth. The point
is, the reason I was so angered by this matter was because a
Gannett reporter told me that he was going to create a story
by misstating the facts. And even with documentation that
he was provided the truth, even with documentation that he
knew the truth, and even with documentation that his editor
knew the truth, he carried through on his promise to create
his perspective without regard for the truth.

These acts were with clear design and purpose. This was no
mistake. The Gannett reporter deliberately misrepresented
the contents of the story before publication (with regard to
inclusion of doctors' pay), deliberately misstated my relative
charges at publication, and deliberately lied to his editor as
to when I was first notified about the story. As a result, my
family, reputation, and practice income suffered.

This was libel:

Libel: n.,

(1) any false and malicious written or printed
statement, or any sign, picture, or effigy,

tending to expose a person to public ridicule, hatred, or contempt, or to injure his reputation in any way

(2) the act of publishing such a thing

Therefore, after being threatened by Corporate Gannett's legal counsel, I immediately sought my own legal counsel. (Being raised in southern Ky., and having gone through a lifetime of obstacles, I must admit having a low tolerance for threats).

Incredibly, however, I was informed by my attorney that although my case had merit, the financial cost and risk to my family and reputation from retribution from Corporate Gannett was too great.

"Gannett's pockets are much deeper than yours."

But at this point, cost didn't matter to me. I was determined in my quest to obtain justice, and was willing to risk my life's savings and future earnings to achieve it. It was my gut feeling that the American judicial system was established to grant justice, irrespective of the parties involved. "All men are created equal." And if the facts were presented before a jury of my piers, I was certain I would be awarded due compensation for loss of income, due compensation for loss of reputation, and due compensation in punitive damages.

But I would soon find yet another roadblock.

INSULATION FROM JUSTICE

After discussing the case with my attorney, I found that the press is substantially insulated from being held accountable, or being responsible for wrongdoings. First of all, although recovering loss of income would probably be successful, the legal costs of a law suit against the multibillion dollar Gannett would vastly exceed any amount I would collect.

Secondly, punitive damages could not be reasonably attainable due to Supreme Court rulings that largely exempts the press from being accountable for their actions. These rulings apparently have created a huge legal loophole allowing the press great latitude in behaving in irresponsible and wrongful ways, without fear of paying damages.

Finally, with regard to loss of reputation, this was next to impossible to quantitate. Hence, regardless of the degree of the atrocities of irresponsible reporting from Gannett, the most I could reasonably expect to recover from loss of reputation would be about $1.

$1.00.

When drafting the First Amendment, I doubt this is exactly

what James Madison had in mind.

Nevertheless, I pressed on. In my view, Gannett had grossly abused the privilege of the "freedom of the press" by using the press as a weapon against individual liberties. And although the easiest route would have been to just give up and drop the matter as recommended, it seemed the least I could do as an American was to sacrifice my time and money for a just cause.

Subsequently, my attorney began negotiations with the Gannett attorney in hopes to settle my claim of libel out of court. Given the prior lack of compassion and remorse at Gannett, I expected absolutely nothing - and was prepared to go to court. However, my attorney was somewhat more successful. He was able to achieve an out of court settlement in which Gannett agreed to a letter of apology. Although I cannot be sure, I suspect his success was partially due to his unique approach in negotiations.

I believe my attorney used a technique perfected by Henry Kissinger during the Nixon administration.

It is my understanding that part of Nixon's foreign policy success was attributable to Kissinger's ability to convince adversaries (such as Russia and China) that Nixon was some kind of wild-man who was capable of just about anything (thermonuclear war, global annihilation, etc.) to achieve his goals.

Hence, these foreign adversaries felt it best to negotiate.

Similarly, I suspect my attorney went to the Gannett

attorney with the argument that, although I had an impeccable academic record, I was also some kind of nut-case for justice, and therefore, just might pursue a libel suit to the bloody end - regardless of the cost.

And he correctly surmised that, although Gannett's pockets were much deeper than mine, apparently they did have seams.

And I must admit, I might have encouraged my attorney's aggressive approach when I told him to inform Gannett that unless they were willing to make some kind of apology, I planned to sue Gannett for the absolute maximum monetary amount of damages for loss of reputation as well as punitive damages.

I planned to sue for $1.00.

$1.00.

Gannett promptly agreed to a letter of apology in a legal settlement. In turn, I agreed to relinquish all future legal challenges against Gannett.

David Hawpe, the lead editor and Vice President, wrote the letter of apology. Upon first reading the letter, I was stunned. After all that had happened I continued to be bewildered and amazed by Gannett. Nowhere in the letter did I perceive any real sense of remorse, or real understanding that the assertion of "innocent until proven guilty" was not just a judicial concept, but rather a representation of a common decency that most folks share. And no where in this letter did I find signs that Gannett felt that it is the dedication to protecting individual liberties through reporting the truth that defines journalism as a profession.

Even my attorney was unimpressed. Noting his disappointment with the wording, my attorney asked if I wished to have the letter revised with "we are sorry for the inaccurate story." After some consideration, I chose to accept the letter "as is." In fact, the more I thought about it, the more content I became. After long thought, I determined that the wording of this letter fulfilled two crucial criteria.

First of all, this letter did fulfill a legal settlement in which Gannett was required to apologize for the wrongdoing on the part of a Gannett reporter. This apology achieved an important goal I had sought from the beginning - a simple acknowledgement of wrongdoing.

But secondly, the choice of words used by a Vice President and Lead Editor of a Gannett newspaper, can leave no doubt as to the shallowness of understanding and compassion of at least one of the leading editors of the press. After the numerous documented lies, after all the intentional misstatements, after all the wrongful pain inflicted on innocent citizens whose only crime was choosing to be doctors in the state of Kentucky, a Vice President and Lead Editor's December 8, 1994 response was:

"The June 4 story was not perfect."

" Few newspaper stories are, often in spite of extraordinary effort on our part. But in

each such instance, including the story at
issue, I am sorry that we didn't do a better
job. I regret any pain that our story caused
you. We will make every effort to avoid any
future problems of this kind."

Wow!

Despite "extraordinary efforts," Gannett regretted that the
story was "not perfect.'

No letter could have been more illustrative of how
out-of-touch newspaper editors are with regard to the
concepts of compassion, atonement, and common decency.
No letter could have been more descriptive of the complete
lack of understanding of the impact an irresponsible reporter
can have on innocent families and reputations. No letter
could have been more confusing to those who have faith in
the ethics of journalists.

For example, when a reporter deliberately lies to the
accused, lies to the editor, and lies to the reader, in what
regard does this represent an "extraordinary effort?"

And if this editor was truly sorry that Gannett "didn't do a
better job," then why did it take over six months of letters
and phone calls, and thousands of dollars of attorney fees
for a lead editor and Vice President of a major newspaper to
admit his sorrow.

If he truly "regretted any pain" that the story caused me,
then why didn't he publicly apologize and retract the errors
on the front page.

And if he truly meant to "make every effort to avoid any

future problems of this kind," then why did he allow the same Gannett reporter, within a matter of weeks after the wrongful story against me, to commit the exact same injustice against my colleagues - simply because they were doctors. Furthermore, why did he fail to fulfill his promise that Gannett would inquire into about my work with the homeless, and my medical directorship of a research center so I could at least regain some of my reputation lost?

So to say that the Gannett story was not "perfect" was somewhat of an understatement. Conversely, his letter was perfect in many ways.

This letter was "perfect" in that it was an example of how many in the press are oblivious to their constitutional obligations. This letter was "perfect" in that it was an example how many in the press are unconcerned as they systematically dismantle individual liberties through abusing and demeaning the intent of the Bill of Rights. And this letter was "perfect" in that it vividly demonstrated that many of the press have forgotten that the origin of the very "freedom of the press" they cherish so much.

Many in the press have forgotten that the Bill of Rights originated from those who sacrificed their lives in their "Unanimous Declaration of the United States of America" that included the time-honored statement:

> "We hold these truths to be self-evident, that all men are created equal, that they are endowed by their Creator with certain unalienable Rights, that among these are Life, Liberty and the pursuit of Happiness."

And because this independence cost so much, most folks truly believe - down in their bones - that all citizens really are created equal, and do have the unalienable right towards the pursuit of happiness, without the fear of wrongful oppression.

Even if their income and prestige may exceed that of the reporter.

At the very least, they are entitled to the truth.

ACCEPTANCE

?

THE PERSPECTIVE

CHAPTER 3:

THIS CAN'T BE HAPPENING IN AMERICA

"How can the press fulfill the constitutional obligation to protect citizen's 'unalienable rights' if they do not respect these rights in their own reporting?"

The Fourteenth Amendment:

Section 1. All persons born or naturalized in the United States and subject to the jurisdiction thereof, are citizens of the United States and of the state wherein they reside. No state shall make or enforce any law which shall abridge the privileges or immunities of citizens of the United States; **nor shall any state deprive any person of life, liberty, or property, without due process of law;** nor deny to any person within its jurisdiction the equal protection of the laws.

THE TEN RULES OF 90' JOURNALISM

It is said that tragedy often gives rise to opportunity. Thus far, I am still trying to find something positive that could justify the pain inflicted on my family and reputation as the result of a significantly fabricated, front page, lead headline story from an irresponsible reporter.

Admittedly, much of what happened was due to my misunderstanding of the mechanics of journalism. My willingness to cooperate with the press worked to my disadvantage. The more I talked, the more my name was reported. If I had made little to no comment, my name would have been reported much less.

My error was in assuming that all who worked in the press were basically decent, hard-working people with the highest level of integrity. I had a mistaken faith that all reporters and editors had an uncompromising dedication to truth, and an unyielding respect and compassion for the reputation of the very citizens they had a constitutional obligation to protect.

And I had wrongfully assumed that it was the dedication to protecting individual liberties through reporting the truth that defines journalism as a profession.

Obviously this was not, and is not, universally true.

But perhaps this book *is* an opportunity to help others avoid the mistakes that I made. Perhaps if even just one person is able to avoid unnecessary harm to family and reputation, then perhaps this, in some small way, makes sense of all of this.

So, for what it is worth, I have listed rules of the press that I think everyone ought to know. Using my experience as a case study, examples are included to illustrate,

"The Ten Rules of 90's Journalism."

I wish I had been given the opportunity to review these rules before May of 1994.

THE TEN RULES OF 90'S JOURNALISM

(1) Perspective matters more than accuracy.

(2) Accused citizens are presumed front page guilty until proven back page innocent.

(3) Constitutional liberties do not apply during trial by the press.

(4) Discriminatory public condemnation of citizens is warranted if the income of those citizens exceed that of the reporter.

(5) "Gotcha" is the most orgasmic word in journalism.

(6) Agenda-minded editorializing and opinion are often given priority over facts when reporting the news.

(7) Although the Constitution grants the press the obligation to use newspapers as a protector of individual liberties, it also grants the press a legal loophole to use newspapers as a weapon against individual liberties.

(8) Apology and atonement for wrongdoing are only required of those on the other side of the First Amendment.

(9) Exposure of specific wrongdoings of corporations, government officials, and citizens is a constitutional obligation; exposure of specific wrongdoings of the corporate press is inappropriate.

(10) Journalism is no longer a profession.

(1) PERSPECTIVE MATTERS MORE THAN ACCURACY.

The Gannett reporter had been sent multiple letters providing him the facts.

The Gannett reporter had been sent a letter confirming that he had the facts.

The Gannett reporter had signed a statement verifying that he had the facts.

The Gannett reporter had reiterated his understanding of the facts in a face-to-face, tape-recorded meeting in the presence of his own editor.

The bottom-line: The Gannett reporter had the facts.

But despite the facts, the Gannett reporter deliberately misstated the facts in order to support his premise. He justified his action by asserting that the specific factual aspects of the story were not nearly as important as the "perspective" of the story. And as a result of achieving his "perspective," my reputation and family were wrongfully harmed.

After the significantly fabricated, front page, lead headline story was reported, I had a face-to-face meeting with the lead editor and vice president of the Gannett Courier-Journal. Reacting as I think most folks would, I was upset. It was my argument that dedication to protecting individual liberties through reporting the truth defines journalism as a profession. Therefore, deliberately misstating the truth was unprofessional journalism. But to my disbelief, the Gannett lead editor and vice president stated that he "somewhat agreed" with the assertion that the perspective was more important than the individual facts of the story.

This was reaffirmed by the Gannett Corporate attorney who indicated his agreement that misstatements are not important as long as the perspective is achieved. In his 10/31/95 letter to persuade me to not to pursue litigation, the Gannett Corporate attorney wrote:

> "That there may have been a minor inaccuracy does not detract from the gist or sting of the story."

He was exactly right.

The "minor" inaccuracies did not *detract* from the sting of the story. In fact, with regard to my reputation and family, it was these very "inaccuracies" that *sharpened* the sting of the story.

I am no journalist. And I might not know the nuances of newspaper reporting. But I do know right from wrong. And if a perspective can only be achieved through lies and deceit, then perhaps the perspective needs re-examination.

(2) CITIZENS ACCUSED OF WRONGDO-ING ARE PRESUMED FRONT PAGE GUILTY UNTIL PROVEN BACK PAGE INNOCENT.

Several weeks after the wrongful attack on my reputation and family, the Gannett reporter then set his sights on other local physicians who cared for the poor. And he again failed to seek reasonable input from the very persons he sought to condemn.

In a repeated demonstration of class warfare, he reported yet another front page, lead headline story of the day that included a chart listing specific amounts that specific doctors supposedly received from Medicaid. The huge headline that was sprawled all across the entire front page was:

> "MEDICAID HAS FIRST MILLION-DOLLAR DOCTOR"

> "EIGHT TOP $500,000 FROM STATE"

This was obviously meant to convey the "perspective" that greedy doctors were pilfering funds that were to have gone to the poor. And, until the true facts were known, he certainly achieved his perspective. Doctors were again the greedy bastards.

"Gotcha."

But it was subsequently revealed that this was blatantly misleading. The payment listed in the chart were in fact *charges* to the state generated by these doctors. The actual *payment* to the doctors was a mere fraction of the charges. And to make matters worse, it was also revealed that this payment did not go directly to the doctors. Instead, the money went to help fund medical clinics for the poor.

Gannett, in the most flagrant example of their pathologic and bizarre obsessions with class warfare, had just condemned those who had dedicated their careers to care for the poor.

"Gotcha?"

The Gannett reporter had again mislead the reader, had failed to give due consideration to the accused, and had wrongfully damaged the reputations of innocent citizens - simply because they were doctors. And it didn't matter that they were doctors who cared for the poor.

That was not his perspective.

As a result of this outrage, even the Gannett Courier-Journal felt compelled to grant a reprieve. The Gannett reporter was required to print a correction regarding the inaccuracies of the listed doctors' incomes. Furthermore, the ombudsman published his objections to this clearly wrongful act in a lengthy, and pointed article. And in an unprecedented event, even the Gannett reporter's colleagues published their disagreement to such journalistic conduct in printed form.

But what about the editors in charge. How "in touch" were they regarding this blatantly wrongful act?

After the Kentucky Medical Association issued a subsequent complaint against Gannett, the Gannett editors responded in a way that could only come from an elite member of the press. In a Gannett Courier-Journal story of September 22, 1994 describing the response of Stephen Ford, this managing editor was quoted as saying that:

> "It was unfortunate that the doctors appeared on the list, but he [Stephen Ford - the managing editor] disagreed with characterizing the story as sloppy journalism. He said a retraction would not be justified."

Not justified?

Inappropriate?

I am not kidding.

Unbelievable.

Time for another definition.

> Sloppy: n.,
>
> (1) Showing lack of care; slovenly or messy
>
> (2) Careless; slipshod

Who else, but someone on that side of the First Amendment, could be so out-of-touch as to believe that repeated misstatements and flat-out lies were not deserving of a retraction? And if the managing editor disagreed that the Gannett reporter's actions could reasonably be characterized as "sloppy," then what would be a reasonable characterization - good, ethical journalism?

This editor may be shocked to discover that most folks feel it is the dedication to protecting individual liberties through reporting the truth that defines journalism as a profession.

Nevertheless, at least the Gannett reporter did correct the wrongful inaccuracies in a follow-up article. He attributed the errors to a "misunderstanding." However, while as this "gotcha" article was displayed as the front page (A1), lead headline story of the day, the correction was buried in section B.

Was this just?

First of all, even if the reporting had been accurate, these doctors had done nothing illegal. Nor had anyone suggested that they did anything unethical. Therefore, other than the pathologic and bizarre obsession to engage in class warfare, why would such a story warrant a front page, lead headline story of the day?

Secondly, the reporting was not accurate. It was grossly inaccurate. The Gannett reporter had yet again been guilty of journalistic unprofessionalism. He had wrongfully harmed innocent citizens with inaccurate reporting for the sole purpose of creating his perspective.

Now, I am no journalist. But why isn't the deliberate and repeated pain inflicted on the families and reputation of innocent citizens by an irresponsible press at least as newsworthy as doctor's incomes? My point is, whenever a wrongful accusation occurs as the front page, lead headline story of the day (Page A1), why does correction of the inaccuracies end up buried in section B?

Those in the press may be shocked to know that most folks on this side of the First Amendment think this is unfair.

And what about me? I experienced a similar injustice, but I did not receive a similar correction. And the misstatements against me were anything but a "misunderstanding."

Why did my case elicit such a different response?

After my face-to-face meeting with the lead editor and vice president of the Gannett Courier-Journal, he promised to help me regain my reputation by having Gannett inquire as to my medical research efforts, as well as my volunteer efforts with the homeless.

I am still waiting.

After the article, I sent Pat Howington - the Gannett reporter - a letter of protest (6/12). I received no phone call, letter, or response.

After the article, I sent Keith Runyon - editor of opinion pages - a "letter to the editor" in two letters of protest (6/12, 6/20). I received no phone call, letter or response.

After the article, I sent Gideon Gill - assistance editor - two letters of protest (6/18, 9/10). I received no phone call, letter, or response.

After the article, I sent Bob Hill - a reporter - a letter of protest (9/10). I received no phone call, letter, or response.

After the article, I sent Stephen Ford - managing editor - a letter of protest (9/25). I received no phone call, letter, or response.

I sent a lot of letters. I received nothing in return except for a threat from the Gannett Corporate attorney.

Now, I am no journalist, but when the reporter and editors shy away from accepting responsibility and/or responding to an article that had just warranted a front page, lead headline story of the day, I've got to wonder what's going on.

And I've got to wonder why wrongful and inaccurate accusations against my colleagues was a front page, lead headline news, while as the truth about my colleagues was back page news.

And I've got to wonder why wrongful and inaccurate accusations against me was front page, lead headline news, while as the truth about the accusations was no news at all.

(3) CONSTITUTIONAL LIBERTIES DO NOT APPLY DURING TRIAL BY THE PRESS.

It is difficult to describe in narrative form the level of emotional stress that occurs to a person and his/her family when a reporter follows through on threats to deliberately report misstatements, irrespective of the potential damage to a lifelong reputation. However, the following letter may give some indication as to how my family and friends were effected.

> "Thursday morning, May 26, I was alone and contently enjoying my life. I was completing the first drafts of two recent studies that I had completed (cholesterol treatment in women and non-insulin drug treatment for high blood sugar in diabetic, hemodialysis patients). But from the moment of your call until our meeting, all things changed... I received phone calls from the Jefferson Co. Medical Society and AMA offering their support. Physician colleagues called to offer their condolences. My wife Dawn, and my office manager Darlene, said they would pray for me. It has been

fascinating to note that the response to an
inquiry from the Courier-Journal has skipped
all the traditional stages of death, and gone
straight to acceptance.''

(May 28, 1994 letter to Gannett reporter, before the article)

....

After the article was published, the Corporate Gannett
attorney suggested that since I was not charged with an
illegal activity, I had no basis for concern. I think this
argument is disingenuous. As stated before, those of us from
smaller communities have great faith and respect for the
press. Therefore, we assume anyone who is the subject of a
front page, lead article has to have done something wrong.
It is not unreasonable to presume that editors and reporters
go through painstaking decision processes, and meticulous
value judgements to ensure that the merits of any story
warrant the potential devastating harm to the subject's
family, business, and reputation - particularly a front page,
lead headline story of the day.

Anyone condemned in a front page lead article must surely
deserve it.

In my case, I had been tried and convicted by a press that
had anointed itself prosecuting attorney, defense attorney,
and judge. And I believe the manner in which the story was
researched, and the manner in which the story was presented
was a gross violation of my individual liberties. Had this
been a trial by jury in a court of law, I would have been
granted basic rights guaranteed by the Bill of Rights. But

since this was trial by the press, I was granted no rights at all.

I wasn't even granted accuracy and fairness.

With this in mind, I wrote a letter to the editor after the significantly fabricated story was published.

It was not published by Gannett.

"Dear Editor,

On 6/4/94, the Courier-Journal published a headline, front page, state-wide, lead story concerning an isolated billing complaint that occurred and was resolved in 1992 at my previous medical practice. 7/4/94 was Independence Day. How would our Founding Fathers view "the freedom of the press" today?

I was first notified about this story through an emergency message on my pager, threatening a one business day opportunity to present my side of a forgotten 2 year old billing complaint. (The Courier-Journal had been working on this story for 3 months). My frantic efforts to track down old records from my previous employer were made more difficult because, as a doctor, I was busy treating patients. During a meeting the following day with the reporter, Pat Howington, I protested this one day opportunity to respond to an isolated billing complaint that took place at another office, AND THAT WAS RESOLVED WITH A REFUND IN 1992 WITHOUT ASSISTANCE OR

INTERVENTION FROM THE PRESS. Mr. Howington denied that such a deadline was given. However, my previous employer also received a fax, documenting a similar threat that the article was to be run in one business day unless a response was made by the end of that day. After committing myself to a hurried and ill-prepared initial response, the Courier-Journal did agree to hold the story for several days, and did allow me a meeting with Gideon Gill, an editor. But had this been a trial by government, I would have been granted the constitutional right of "due process of law" with regard to time to recover and review all the facts (5th Amendment), and been granted the time to have "the assistance of counsel" from colleagues before being required to respond (6th Amendment).

Nonetheless, I fully cooperated with the Courier-Journal, who still chose to misstate the facts. It was reported that the bill "was $200 for the office visit, almost six times the $35 that an internist had charged her the year before." However, it was later correctly reported that in 1992, I reduced the fee to $97. Furthermore, the internist received $75, not $35, as was clearly stated in a letter from the patient herself. I repeatedly emphasized this very point to the reporter in conversations and in letters before the article was published. Although comparing $200 to $35 was more sensational, the payment of $97 for my initial, complex evaluation, and the payment of $75 for her internist's initial, brief evaluation was the documented truth. Had this been a trial by government, I would have been granted "due process of law" (5th Amendment).

Mr. Howington even admitted that he knew of no physician who had been more cooperative and forthcoming with personal records. I did this because, as stated in a letter to Mr. Howington, "I do not fear the truth. I have all confidence that you will be factual." I then released a statement regarding my income. Because my practice focuses on cognitive skills such as education and counseling, preventive medicine, as well as a highly trained office staff, I thought it relevant that my income was simply not high enough to be a viable issue for class condemnation by the Courier-Journal. Furthermore, I spend a great deal of time writing research papers and performing volunteer work. The result is that after 4 years of College, 4 more years in Medical School, 3 more years in Internal Medicine Residency, 2 more years in Endocrinology and Metabolism Fellowship, and despite being board certified in both Internal Medicine and Endocrinology (having scored among the top in the nation on both exams), despite being elected to the Fellowship of the American College of Physicians, despite 5 years of medical practice, despite seeing 15 - 20 of among the most complicated patients a day, and despite being on call 24 hours a day (except every other weekend), my pre-tax income through the practice (minus corporate loans) netted $37,778 for the previous 12 months. However, I was told that this information was not relevant since "the story" did not pertain to doctors' incomes. I therefore agreed that my income should not be included. Imagine my surprise when the article was published and included a large chart with the heading "DOCTOR'S PAY," listing the incomes of physicians. Had this been a trial by government, I would have been "informed of the nature and cause of the accusation" (6th Amendment).

Mr. Howington justified "the story" because he felt the perspective mattered more than a comprehensive discussion of this single incident. But I had no desire to be a "perspective," especially since it was my name on the page. Was the "perspective" that I am a bad doctor? The Courier-Journal neglected my numerous academic awards and achievements. They ignored my publications in major worldwide medical journals. They failed to mention that I direct free study programs for minorities, women, and other persons with metabolic disorders such as high cholesterol, diabetes, and hypertension. Was the "perspective" that I am an unethical doctor? The Courier-Journal failed to mention my longstanding physician volunteer work for homeless men, as well as that I personally have helped raised tens of thousands of dollars for charities such as Persons with AIDS, cancer, arthritis, United Negro College Fund, and the American Diabetes Association for which I was the citywide, fund-raising winner of the 1992 "Kiss a Pig" contest.

Our forefathers established the Bill of Rights to protect citizens against oppressive dictatorial institutions that, in their zeal and arrogance, felt justified in discarding individual liberties. We Americans have believed that certain "unalienable rights" should not be violated, even if violations of these rights are perceived to benefit the majority at large. The 14th Amendment has required that the Bill of Rights be honored by all states. Hence, slavery, political censorship, and unfair legal practices have been abolished for all citizens, regardless of race, gender, and/or occupation.

These constitutional rights ensure that, during trial by the government, justice is blind. It does not matter that I am a doctor, because my liberties are equally protected as a doctor as when I was a busboy, dishwasher, janitor, cook, and clerk at Food Mart. But during trial by the Courier-Journal, justice was not blind. It very much mattered that I was a doctor. And because I was a doctor, the Courier-Journal denied me accurate reporting with regard to "due process," and denied me truthful information regarding "the nature and cause of the accusation." Instead, an isolated billing complaint from a disgruntled patient who (as in Mr. Howington's words) "changes doctors as often as some people change hairdressers," was published in a front page, huge headline, state-wide, lead article, regardless that it was over 2 years old, regardless that it occurred in a previous practice, and regardless that it was voluntarily resolved in 1992 with a refund of $103. Weighing the merits of this 1992 "story" against the potentially devastating harm to my family and reputation, I think reasonable persons might have agreed that this violated my rights against "excessive fine imposed, or cruel and unusual punishment inflicted" (8th Amendment).

And I realize that the Courier-Journal did not intend that this be perceived as a front page crime story. (The names of persons convicted of actual crimes such as maiming their spouse, rape, robbery, and other assorted hooliganisms were buried on page infinitum in the "You'll Never See It" section of the newspaper). But the manner in which "the story" was researched, and the deliberate manner in which the facts were misstated sure made it feel like a crime story. And I also realize that the First Amendment virtually exempts the press from any legal obligations to honor the rights of individuals. But how can the press fulfill the constitutional obligation to protect citizen's "unalienable rights" if they do not respect these rights in their own reporting? Have we reached the point where citizens can expect greater protection of "life, liberty, and the pursuit of happiness" from the government than from the press?

And what do we make of the preoccupation towards stirring class anger towards health care providers? In this article, the Courier-Journal listed the chart of incomes of doctors; but no accompanying chart of the effort and sacrifice that may justify these incomes. Where was the chart listing the income of other upper income persons, such as newspaper owners? Also, a plea was made for any patient with any gripe to contact the Courier-Journal to expose evil doctors; but no similar plea was made for patients to contact the Courier-Journal for positive experiences. Furthermore, the Courier-Journal has been a consistent mouthpiece for the government in their support of a discriminatory "sin" tax on health care providers, designed to free up money for the spending spree of the politicians. The point is, although I respect that the editors and the politicians may share the same agenda, and therefore similar opinions, why do these opinions occupy space in the reporting section, rather than the editorial section of the newspaper?

Some of my colleagues have expressed fear that, by taking a stand with this letter, I would antagonize the press - even if it accurately reflects my feelings, as well as the feelings of many other physicians. I share these fears as I now know, firsthand, the health care vigilantism that has become a hallmark of today's media. But at some point, someone has to ask the Courier-Journal to please end this war against good, decent, hard-working people, and consider the possibility that doctors and other health care providers may be no less ethical than reporters and editors. If a physician is guilty of a crime, then so be it. Print the details. But if I have dedicated and sacrificed most of my life to patient care, to academia, and to helping those less fortunate in the community, I believe my family and I have earned the right to be allowed an occasional billing dispute without condemnation by my hometown newspaper - regardless of the of perceived value of "the story."

I may be a doctor; but I am still a citizen, and have no less rights than when I was a janitor."

H. Bays M.D., F.A.C.P.

(4) DISCRIMINATORY PUBLIC CONDEMNATION OF CITIZENS WITH SELECTED OCCUPATIONS IS WARRANTED IF THE AVERAGE INCOME OF THOSE OCCUPATIONS EXCEED THAT OF THE REPORTER.

The Gannett Courier-Journal has a long history of a pathologic and bizarre obsession to engage in class warfare against doctors. For example, in another front page, lead headline story about doctors in 1992, it was stated,

> "ARE HANDSOME PROFITS, HIGH INCOMES CROSSING LINE INTO PROFITEERING?"

In this article, the Gannett reporter included a chart with the,

> "Incomes, Net Worths of Selected Kentucky Health-Care Providers."

This chart not only included the numerical amounts of income and net worth of 11 area doctors, but also had the accompanying pictures of the selected doctors.

Yes, I said net worth and pictures.

The Courier - Journal

Are handsome profits, high incomes crossing line into profiteering?

By ROBERT T. GARRETT
Staff Writer

What kinds of incomes do health-care providers in Kentucky command? Is profiteering in the industry a problem?

SECOND STORY

Directly to the right of the front page, lead story of the day was a 1992 story about "Ethnic Cleansing." Earlier that year, Serbian nationalists, with unabated military expansionism, began a policy of eliminating rival Muslims and Croats, often through unspeakable atrocities.

This article details how two orphans were killed by Serbian snipers while on a bus-ride to Germany.

Serbian officials, by using names as the sole manner of segregation, then forced Serbian children to stay in a Serbian-controlled suburb, while as the children that were deemed of other nationalities were required to continue their journey.

FRONT PAGE, LEAD HEADLINE STORY OF THE DAY

The lead story "Are handsome profits, high incomes crossing line into profiteering?" made no specific allegations of wrongdoing, illegal acts, or unethical behavior. It simply listed the incomes of specific doctors (as well as their pictures) with the intent to portray doctors as greedy bastards. The information for the story was obtained through divorce records, etc.

QUESTIONS

These doctors had done nothing illegal. Their only "crime" was their income. The use of divorce records was cruel. The listing of income associated with pictures was unusual, as the income of other highly paid persons, such as Gannett editors and corporate executives have yet to be listed in a front page story. Was this a violation of The Eighth Amendment of the Constitution that grants the right to not be subject to "cruel and unusual punishments inflicted?"

Why is the report of income of doctors of more journalistic merit, and of a greater atrocity than the killing of orphans in a systematic policy of "Ethnic Cleansing?"

And how did the reporter obtain such information?

He acquired this information from lawsuits involving disclosure of personal finances - such as divorce settlements.

I am not kidding.

Unbelievable.

Get out of here "right to privacy."

And to squelch any doubts as to Gannett's pathological, and bizarre obsession to engage in class envy, one only needs to look to the article which included the following,

> "With populist overtones, reformers say that ordinary Kentuckians know profiteering is a problem - not from statistics, but because they have seen the providers' fancy cars in the reserved parking spaces at medical buildings and have at least heard of their private planes, fancy boats, and posh houses."

Yeah! Forget the statistics! Doctors need to be slammed regardless of the facts! Lets string em' up!

Such reporting does not help solve problems, nor does it help protect individual liberties. If a doctor, or anyone, is thought guilty of "profiteering," then specific acts of misconduct should be reported.

Let me rephrase that.

If a doctor, or anyone, is thought guilty of "profiteering," then specific acts of misconduct should be *truthfully* reported. But to condemn anyone of wrongdoing solely on the basis of income is wrong.

Another problem with the kind of class warfare conducted by the Gannett Courier-Journal, as well as their comrades in state government, is that class envy costs jobs.

A few years ago, the Kentucky legislature discovered that in order to continue their past pork spending, and to create new pork projects, they needed to find more money to fund Medicaid, the government-ran health program for the poor.

Where, oh where, could they get the money?

Well, cigarettes had been subject to a "sin tax," because cigarette smoking was known to contribute to health care costs, and was thus a "sin." And sinful acts deserve discriminatory taxation.

Alcohol had been subject to a "sin tax" because excessive alcohol consumption was known to contribute to health care costs, and was thus a "sin." And sinful acts deserve discriminatory taxation.

By the same rationale, those who provided health care were also contributing to health care costs, and were therefore "sinful."

And sinful people deserve discriminatory taxation.

Thus a provider "sin" tax was born. At the date of this writing, Kentucky required that all doctors and hospitals be taxed 2% of gross income to help pay for society's responsibility of health care for the poor. In order for the Kentucky legislature to sell this concept, physicians and hospitals were told that the federal government would match those funds taxed by providers, and Medicaid reimbursement to health care providers would be increased accordingly. Everyone would win.

However, the state government pulled the switch. Not only did Medicaid reimbursement not increase, but after the provider tax was passed, the state government attempted to reduce reimbursement to health care providers.

Physicians had trusted the government.

Mistake.

As a result, those in the health care field were levied a discriminatory tax based not on level of income, but solely on occupation.

This type of taxation was wrong on many levels.

First of all, providing health care was not, and is not a sin. Providing health care to the poor is a desirable, societal responsibility. The payment of such care should no more be shouldered by those who provide health care than anyone else. However, if it is truly a principled position that those who help provide a public service should be taxed to help pay for the service rendered, then lets take other examples. Should teachers be levied a 2% tax on their gross income to pay for education? Should police officers be levied a 2% tax on their gross income to pay for crime prevention? Should groceries be levied a 2% tax on their gross income to pay for food for the hungry? Should newspapers be levied a 2% tax on their gross income to educate the illiterate?

Secondly, taxation to provide a societal responsibility should not be based on occupation. This is discrimination.

However, if it was truly a principled position that those of higher income should have been taxed more to help provide health care to the poor, then taxes should have been increased on all wealthy persons and wealthy corporations, not just those in the health care field. For example, perhaps the Gannett Co. and Gannett editors could have kick in a few bucks of their substantial wealth.

Thirdly, Gannett and the state government somehow forgot that physicians and hospitals already had taken large cuts in pay by agreeing to see Medicaid patients. Reimbursement to care for such patients paid pennies on the dollar. However, despite the loss of income, many of us continued to see Medicaid patients anyway, because we thought it was the right thing to do.

I wonder how grocery store owners would react if they could sell a loaf of bread to regular customers for $1.00, but were required by the government to sell the same loaf of bread to the poor for $0.50? How would car dealerships react if they could sell a car to regular customers for $15,000, but were required by the government to sell the same car to the poor for $7,000? How would Gannett react if they could sell advertising space to regular customers for $500, but were required by the government to sell the same space to the poor for $250? And I wonder how all of these folks would react if after agreeing to pennies on the dollar reimbursement, they were also levied an additional 2% tax on gross income.

Also, the provider "sin" tax was calculated on the gross income, not net income. This means that the medical practices with the most overhead were the most taxed. Since procedures are mostly conducted in hospitals, this meant that the tax fell hardest on non-procedurally based practices such as primary care doctors. As such, since primary care doctors often require expensive overhead (sometimes exceeding 50%), then this 2% tax became a 5 - 10% tax on net income. And this tax was in addition to corporate taxes, employee taxes, employer Medicare taxes, employer Social Security taxes, personal income taxes, personal state taxes, personal local taxes, sales taxes, and an assortment of malpractice insurance "taxes" required in order to practice medicine.

The point is, doctors already paid plenty of taxes.

Finally, the tax was applied to all doctors, even if they did not see Medicaid patients. Hence, the provider tax was nothing more than a discriminatory, occupational tax that unfairly burdened health care providers to pay for a social responsibility, and unfairly punished a segment of Kentuckians based on their unfortunate choice of choosing health care as their occupation.

So after consideration of all the above, what position did the Gannett Courier-Journal take? Did they choose principle? Or did they engage in yet another example of their pathologic, and bizarre obsession with class warfare against doctors?

Need I even ask?

Of course Gannett thought the provider tax was a great idea because it was a way to increase funding for health care for the poor without affecting Gannett's financial bottom line.

They loved it.

Think of it. The Kentucky legislature had found a way to pay for health care for the poor without taxing the enormous wealth of the Gannett editors, publishers, and corporation at large. And best of all, the payment of a societal responsibility was achieved by imposing a discriminatory "sin" tax on evil health care providers.

Thus, Gannett had fulfilled two more "perspectives." It had fulfilled the financial perspective that someone else other than Gannett should pay for health care for the poor. And it fulfilled the health care vigilantism perspective that evil health care providers were the best candidate.

This was the perfect solution.

The Gannett editorials, in that they supported and promoted a tax that directly improved the bottom-line of editors, publishers, and Gannett corporate officials, had transformed a newspaper that was once based on principle, into a financial newsletter based on promoting self-serving, corporate interests.

And as a result of their support for the provider tax, and as the result of the hostile attacks on the health care industry by Gannett and the Kentucky legislature, Columbia HCA, the largest hospital chain in the world, was forced to move its headquarters from Louisville Ky. to Nashville Tennessee.

Consequently, over 600 well-paying jobs were lost.

The presence of Columbia HCA in the state of Kentucky

generated income and prestige to the state. Furthermore, having Columbia HCA's headquarters in Kentucky increased tax revenues that helped fund needed state programs. But because of the unprincipled, unfair, and discriminatory attitudes of Gannett, as well as the Kentucky legislature, this major industry was lost.

Afterwards, I wrote this letter to the editor. I did not mail it.

Dear Editor,

What is the lesson of the move of Columbia HCA?

High paying jobs and industries bring prosperity to a state. High paying jobs and industries increase tax revenue to help pay for programs for the poor, as well as projects that increase the quality of life for all Kentuckians. And high paying jobs and industries are often run by prosperous businesses and prosperous business owners. Prosperous-minded states welcome prosperity. Poor-minded states punish prosperity.

Tennessee understands. Kentucky does not.

Kentucky, through a discriminatory "sin" tax on health care providers, along with the Gannett Courier-Journal's repeatedly inaccurate class warfare attacks on health care providers, have successfully punished the prosperous health care industry in an act of health care vigilantism. Columbia HCA has now been successfully persuaded to move to Tennessee -along with their 600 jobs.

In my early years as a busboy, dishwasher, cook and janitor, I made less money than the business owners for whom I worked. In retrospect, I am now thankful that these businesses did not become more successful. If they had become more prosperous, the state government and the Gannett Courier-Journal would likely have tried to convince me that my more wealthy employers were deserving of unfair discriminatory taxation, and unfair public humiliation. And my hunger to punish these "evil" businesses and business owners would have been satisfied when my employers were successfully forced to move to another state.

And I would have lost my job.

What is the lesson of the move of Columbia HCA? The lesson to businesses considering the creation of well-paying jobs in Kentucky is simple: If you aspire to failure and/or mediocrity, Kentucky is a wonderful state. But if you aspire to prosperity, go elsewhere.

I have heard Gannett reporters on the local cable network discuss the provider tax. The shallowness of their principles was frightening. But after my experience with Gannett, it was not particularly surprising. When one particular Gannett reporter was asked why doctors (based on principle) should be levied a discriminatory occupational tax to fund a societal responsibility, the reporter said,

"Hey, nobody likes to pay taxes."

That was his level of insight. This is a typical Gannett

Courier-Journal response to a question of principle.

What hypocrisy.

If Gannett truly feels that citizens are worthy of condemnation and discriminatory taxation based solely on income, net worth, and occupation, then where are all the stories about the income and net worth of Gannett's editors and owners? As long as Gannett maintains their pathologic and bizarre obsession with incomes of other occupations, I challenge Gannett to periodically publish the net worth and income of those editors and owners affiliated with Gannett.

ANNUAL INCOMES OF OCCUPATIONS AFFILIATED WITH JOURNALISM [1]

Newspaper Reporters.. . . . . $26,700 - $45,400 [2]

Managing Editors. . . . . > $60,000 [2]

Vice President and Editor. . . . . $60,000 - $700,000 [3]

President and Publisher . . . . $60,000 - $700,000 [3]

Division President of Gannett. . . . . $ 707,806 [4]

Chief Financial Officer of Gannett . . . . $1,152,894 [4]

Chief Executive Officer of Gannett. . . . $1,351,452 [4]

Television Newscasters . . . . Millions

----

1. May not include benefits such as health insurance, retirement, stock options, private planes, corporate perks, etc.

2. According to 1992 statistics from the "Occupational Outlook Handbook" U.S. Department of Labor. Bureau of Labor Statistics May 1994

3. Estimate based on income range between Managing Editor and Gannett Corporate Executives.

4. Based on 1994 publicly released figures (see references).

Wouldn't revealing this information bring objectivity to stories that engage in class warfare? Would this not bring balance to the story? Would this not serve the public good?

But I guess Gannett feels that income alone is worthy of front page condemnation only if it is earned by those on the other side of the First Amendment.

(5) "GOTCHA" IS THE MOST ORGASMIC WORD IN JOURNALISM

The Gannett reporter had distinguished himself as the kind of reporter who allowed nothing to stand in the way of "getting his story" - even if those things happen to be accuracy, integrity, and ethical journalism.

But, I was not involved in the "Pelican Brief."

And, I was not the one-armed man.

Yet I was the recipient of what has become the equivalent of journalistic phone sex. On a fateful Thursday afternoon, the Gannett reporter called me to say:

"Gotcha."

It was only after the Gannett reporter had been writing the story for three months, and only after he had a personal interview with the accuser three weeks prior, that he suddenly threatened me with a single business day to comment on an isolated two year old billing complaint that occurred while I was an employee at another practice - an event for which I had no recollection.

Consequently, I was forced to make frantic efforts to track

down two year old records from my previous employer. And to make matters worse, my day-long commitment to study patients, office patients, and hospital patients, grossly limited my ability to review the necessary documents. I had no time to seek assistance or counsel with the local Medical Society. I had no time to seek legal counsel to assist me in dealing with such a reporter.

And as hard as it may be for journalists to understand, many doctors such as myself do not have full-time, or even part-time press secretaries, investigative departments, and legal teams. Many doctors, such as myself, tend to focus their practice on treating patients.

Hence, I was totally unprepared to handle this assault.

After the article, I protested such bully tactics to the lead editor and vice president of the Gannett Courier-Journal. The editor stated "we don't do that." He sternly stated that the "gotcha" investigative mentality is not tolerated at the Gannett Courier-Journal. Furthermore, he showed me a computer print out provided to him "documenting" that I had been sent a letter and had received phone calls about this matter for three weeks before publication of the story - all of which I ignored.

It was clear that this was yet another fabrication.

It was clear that the Gannett reporter had not only lied to the reader about my relative office charges, had not only lied to me about the story's content regarding doctor's pay, but it was now clear that the Gannett reporter had flat-out lied to his editor as to when I was notified of the story.

I then provided documentation to support that I had in fact not been notified sooner. I provided him countless letters and documented phone calls, and closed my argument with:

> "In your brief experience with me, do I seem like someone who chooses to ignore the press?"

Prior to my face-to-face meeting with this editor, I'm not sure I had ever heard of, and much less understood the mentality of "gotcha." But ever since becoming acquainted with this terminology, I have found this code word used in journalistic talk shows, as well as movies about journalism.

I have come to realize that the "gotcha" phone call is among the most desired thrills of investigative journalism.

It is now my belief that during the "gotcha" phone call, the Gannet reporter experienced great frustration when he discovered that the facts did not support his premise. His "gotcha" ecstasy was ruined.

He had experienced "gotcha interruptus."

And as such, he likely felt as though reality had rang the doorbell right during the climax of his "gotcha" phone fantasy.

And he wasn't pleased about it.

But while as I appreciate the primordial needs of investigative journalists, I believe the "gotcha" technique compromises justice. And I brought up this very point to the lead editor and vice president of the Gannett Courier-Journal. I brought up the Fifth Amendment.

It was my argument that the demand of immediate response through intimidation no more serves justice during trial by press, than during trial by jury. And had I known that the press was capable of the degree of deceit demonstrated by Gannett, and had I been given Fifth Amendment considerations, I would likely have received counsel and possibly would have responded with:

> "This patient was seen while I was an employee at another practice. I have no recollection of her case. I have no further comment."

Consequently, my public condemnation would have been far less. And my name would certainly not have been cited 11 times. In other words, without the "gotcha" orgasmic, bully tactics of Gannett, my family and reputation would have undergone far less harm.

(6) AGENDA-MINDED EDITORIALIZING AND OPINION ARE OFTEN GIVEN PRIORITY OVER FACTS WHEN REPORTING THE NEWS.

Much has been said about the "liberal media." It is said that the editorial boards of many newspapers are of liberal bias.

But I make a distinction between "irresponsible liberalism" and "responsible liberalism." "Responsible liberalism" seeks to challenge all citizens to take personal responsibility in the unwavering defense of individual liberties, irrespective of race, gender, religion, or political ideology. "Irresponsible liberalism" attacks and dismantles individual liberties of citizens based on race (advocating "reverse discrimination"), gender ("male bashing"), religion (hatred of the "religious right"), and ideology (characterizing conservatives as mean-spirited, "extra chromosome," starvers of small children). Furthermore, those who engage in "irresponsible liberalism" frolic in the opportunity to trample on the individual liberties of selected citizens, based solely on occupation or income, or on promotion of an agenda or "perspective."

In the case of the Gannett Courier-Journal, this has certainly been common-place after the departure of the influence of the Binghams.

For example, the following is an excerpt of a Gannett Courier-Journal editorial of Feb. 11, 1995,

> "From all the evidence.., Dr. ____ is an extraordinarily, decent man with an exemplary record of community service and professional accomplishment... He should be basking in near universal acclaim for his many successes. Instead, he's being vilified as a devil... His mistake? Believing that the clear, honorable reality of his life's work would count for something... But reality doesn't count for much, at least among the zealots who dominate our public life these days... It is the assault on Dr.____ that is the abomination..."
>
> "Dr. ____'s record, conduct and beliefs embody exactly the vital responsible center.., and we hope the (people) get the chance...to see him and his critics for what they really are."

This doctor had committed no illegal act. Nevertheless, his stellar reputation had fallen victim to a lead-story condemnation, based solely on an isolated issue. The editors demanded that this doctor be allowed an opportunity to correct these misleading reports in a public forum, and to respond to the "zealots who dominate our public life."

Promoting a perspective or agenda by publicly demonizing

individuals through a front page, inaccurate report of a single issue, particularly when no crime was committed, is among the most cruelest acts against individual liberties. And to harm individuals through admittedly inaccurate reporting of a single event, without allowing a public airing of the individual's "life's work" is among the most painful acts against citizens and their families.

Therefore, I fully agreed with the Gannett Courier-Journal editorial comments. But, this editorial was not about me, it was about Dr. Henry W. Foster - President Clinton's nominee for Surgeon General. And perhaps therein lied the problem. Perhaps I would have received the same consideration given to this out-of-town doctor if I had received prior approval by someone on the political left.

Or perhaps I would have received similar considerations if at some point in my medical career, I had performed a few abortions.

And to be clear, this is not to criticize the right of Gannett to take a position on abortion. The abortion issue is a very controversial subject that has too often been raised, not for thoughtful dialogue regarding the role of government, but as a divisive wedge issue raised for political gain.

The Ninth Amendment states,

> "The enumeration in the Constitution, of certain rights, shall not be construed to deny or disparage others retained by the people."

It should be noted that a "right to abortion" or a "right to privacy" is not specifically stated in this Ninth Amendment to the Bill of Rights. However, it is in this Ninth Amendment that the Supreme Court has recognized the "right to privacy" in its support of the Roe v. Wade decision.

And beyond the courts, many reasonable, religious folks agree with "the right to privacy," when the decision of an abortion is made to save the life of the mother. Many feel that such decisions are difficult and emotional enough without having the government involved.

For example, if it is found through prenatal testing that the fetus of a pregnant mother has a horrible genetic abnormality with no chance of survival, or with no chance of survival much beyond birth, and if it is advised by a physician that continued pregnancy poses a health risk to the life of the mother, many feel that the very difficult decision whether abortion is appropriate should be that of the mother and father, not the government. In this case, the decisions of undergoing a medically recommended procedure does not have a clear right or wrong ethical answer. As such, it becomes an individual judgement that is the "right" of the parents to decide, based upon their individual moral and spiritual values.

Others who have never been through this experience may disagree. But such honest disagreements should not be decided in law.

At the same time, if the unborn child has no condition that would impair a reasonable chance of survival, I think most folks would agree that abortion should not be performed simply as method of birth control, or to choose the gender of a child. Therefore, most folks believe that the "right to privacy" should exist, but with some restrictions.

However, many in the press resist *any* limits on the "right to privacy" interpretation of the Ninth Amendment. Many in the press believe that the principle of the "right to privacy" should be not be abridged, even if it means the death of a healthy, unborn child.

Fine. The press has the constitutional freedom to print such opinions. But if those in the press are so adamant about the "right to privacy" regarding such a fuzzy and controversial issue such as abortion, why are they not equally unwavering in their defense of "right to privacy" when it comes to other issues, such as reporting a citizen's income. Quite frankly, my income is nobody's business but my own. And it is most certainly not the business of a press who feels justified in winding up the Ninth Amendment only when it suits their political bias.

Either believe in the "right to privacy" or don't.

The point is, most folks believe that the "perspective" of any issue in the news section should be based on truth, and a foundation of principle, rather than the biases or political leanings of newspaper editors. And to take this one step further, most folks would agree that any issue in the editorial section should also be based on truth and consistency of principle.

But it is the inconsistency of principle that is often the rule with many in the press. Some might even describe the editorial positions of the press as hypocritical at times - i.e. without a consistent, underlying principle. In this case, Gannett believed that "the right to privacy" justified any abortions that Dr. Foster may have committed. And they printed as such in the editorial section. However, their repeated front page, lead story attacks (often significantly fabricated) concerning incomes of doctors would not be consistent with a belief in the "right to privacy." And these front page attacks were not editorials; they were suppose to represent unbiased reporting.

In my judgement, if the editors must be inconsistent in their principles (and feel the need to be reckless with the truth) in order to achieve their political "perspectives," at least restrict these opinions in the editorial section. It is the editorial section that is the most appropriate section to promote personal agendas - not the news section.

The flagship Gannett newspaper - the USA Today - also has an editorial section with a stated goal attributed to Allen H. Neuharth - Founder, Sept. 15, 1982. His goal is reprinted in each issue of USA Today. It states,

> "USA TODAY hopes to serve as a forum
> for better understanding and unity to help
> make the USA truly one nation."

This is a lofty goal in a society with so many differing opinions. But to help us understand all sides of an issue, the Gannett USA Today routinely expresses their opinion editorials with the label,

> "Our view."

The Gannett USA Today routinely also expresses opposing opinion editorials published at the same time, on the same page with the label,

> "Opposing view."

In this way, Gannett can rightly and fairly present their political bias, because it is counter-balanced with another opinion. And because the real truth for just about everyone is probably in, around or somewhere between these opinions, it can be reasonably assumed that USA Today is indeed serving as a forum for better understanding and unity.

But the Gannett Courier-Journal does not allow such opposing views. And their goal and conduct has precious little regard for unity. In fact, the goal of the Gannett Courier-Journal editorials might best be stated as,

> "The Courier-Journal hopes to serve as a forum for our editors to express their petty, narrow-minded, pointy-headed viewpoints to help make Kentucky one divided, neurotic, messed up little state."

Think about it. If a poll were taken to determine the validity of these 10 rules of 90's journalism, I suspect that the majority of folks would agree that most, if not all of these rules accurately describe today's press.

- (1) Perspective matters more than accuracy.
- (2) Accused citizens are presumed front page guilty until proven back page innocent.
- (3) Constitutional liberties do not apply during trial by the press.

- (4) Discriminatory public condemnation of citizens is warranted if the income of those citizens exceed that of the reporter.

- (5) "Gotcha" is the most orgasmic word in journalism.

- (6) Agenda-minded editorializing and opinion are often given priority over facts when reporting the news.

- (7) Although the Constitution grants the press the obligation to use newspapers as a protector or individual liberties, it also grants the press a legal loophole to use newspapers as a weapon against individual liberties.

- (8) Apology and atonement for wrongdoing is required only of those on the other side of the First Amendment.

- (9) Exposure of specific wrongdoings of corporations, government officials, and citizens is a constitutional obligation; exposure of specific wrongdoings of the corporate press is inappropriate.

- (10) Journalism is no longer a profession.

And when newspapers such as the Gannett Courier-Journal conduct themselves in a manner that elicits these feelings among their readers, how does this help achieve unity?

And when newspapers such as the Gannett Courier-Journal conduct themselves in class warfare (such as health care vigilantism), how does this help achieve unity?

And when newspapers such as the Gannett Courier-Journal systematically dismantle individual liberties for the sake of creating a perspective, how does this help achieve unity?

And when newspapers such as the Gannett Courier-Journal fail to accept the responsibility for deliberate wrongful acts of their reporters, despite how "minor" they think these inaccuracies may be, how does this help achieve unity?

This does not help achieve unity. It is divisive.

And worst of all, it affects the manner in which the news is reported.

When editors express divisive attitudes, this does not go unnoticed by reporters that are assigned to report the news. In order to "please" the editors, the reporter may seek to fulfill the predetermined "perspective" of his/her editors in investigative reports - even if it means reporting misstatements and trampling liberties.

For example, during my first conversation with the Gannett reporter, I inquired as to why doctors were being vilified with inaccurate reporting while as true abuses of health care were being ignored. I brought up an example of what I thought accurately represented an inequity in the entitlement program Medicaid. I described an event that took place in early 1994, at a local hospital.

On a particular morning while doing my hospital rounds, I arrived on one of the hospital floors. Upon reviewing my patients' charts, I felt a distinct sense of anger and frustration among many of the nursing staff.

This was unusual.

These nurses, as most nurses, were typically a cheery and professional group. And for those not accustomed to the health care system, nursing is among the true professions in our society - from an academic, as well as altruistic standpoint.

Academically, nurses have among the most strenuous undergraduate requirements (higher than most journalists I might add). In addition, postgraduate nursing school requires even more rigorous, high-level training.

Because of the lack of income during education and training, and because of the need for loans to fund education and training, many nurses experience financial difficulty. Even after becoming employed, it may be years before they become financially sound.

This creates a hardship on nurses of either gender. But because many (and still most) nurses continue to be women, and because women have societal and biological uniqueness, this often involves personal sacrifices of women that have not been discussed enough. Societally, it often creates difficulties when a professional woman's pay represents the major source of income in the family. And it may create particular difficulty when a professional woman's pay represents the only source of income in the family.

(It is amazing how many professional nurses are married to out-of-work, do-nothing husbands whose only goal in life is (1) to drink and fish with their friends, (2) to wait for dinner to be prepared by their working wives, and (3) to try and find a doctor who will approve that disability check).

But despite the financial constraints, most nurses express an unrestrained sense of caring that is every much as important in healing as doctors orders. Due to these enormous financial demands, and the enormous personal demands inherent in nursing, sacrifices, by necessity, are often made.

One major sacrifice for women nurses is the self limitation of child-bearing. Again, because of financial, time and professional sacrifices, many women nurses must forego having children until later years - and thus often limit the total number of children they conceive.

And make no mistake, many women nurses would dearly love to have more children. However, because of their desire to be the best parents they can, they make the sacrifice in a selfless act of personal responsibility.

Which brings us back to the hospital.

After a few minutes, I asked the nurses why they were so upset. They indicated their disbelief that a long-time Medicaid recipient with three healthy children had just been admitted to their floor.

Knowing that Medicaid patients were often admitted to this floor, I was confused. These nurses had never before displayed anything but professionalism towards any admitted patient. These nurses had never displayed differing levels of care or concern to any patient based upon socio-economic status, ability to pay, or insurance status.

What was so different about this Medicaid admission?

As it turns out, this abled-bodied, unmarried, unemployed, long-time Medicaid recipient (who already had conceived three children being raised in an environment of governmental dependency) was being admitted to have her tubal ligation reversed such that she might conceive yet more children. And not only were tax-payer dollars funding the hospital admission and operation, but tax-payer dollars would also be required to fund the total care of all future children conceived.

To most folks, it is not hard to understand the frustration of these nurses. Their hard-earned tax dollars were funding a system that demanded limits on those who sacrifice their lives to work, but accepted no limits on the riches of child-bearing to those who chose not to work.

After relating this story to the Gannett reporter, he clearly did not share the opinions of these professional women. He indicated that in his view, this Medicaid woman should have the right to have more children, even if she remained unemployed. And not only was she entitled to more children at tax-payers expense, but she also was entitled to tax-payer funding of her hospital admission and reversal of her tubal ligation in order to facilitate her ability to have more children.

In what has to be the most twisted logic I have ever encountered, he stated that he felt "uncomfortable" about giving the government "the choice" of how many children women should conceive.

This is the kind of irresponsible liberalism that drives working tax-payers absolutely nuts.

How devoid of compassion does one have to be to make this assessment? Or, to use a Phil Gramm analogy, how can it be justified to accept limits on families of a professional, tax-paying woman who helps *pull the wagon,* while as is unacceptable to limit the family number of a government-sustained, healthy woman who *rides in the wagon* - especially if she already has three children.

I began to realize that, for the first time in my life, I had met a humanoid being (i.e. a reporter), clearly from a different world.

But even after this conversation, and even after establishing an obvious polarization in our political viewpoints, I did not realize how this might effect the Gannett's reporting of the news. After all, he was not suppose to be writing an editorial about me. He was writing a front page, lead headline story of the day. And because it is the dedication to protecting individual liberties through reporting the truth defines journalism as a profession, our political viewpoints would have no bearing on the eventual story.

I was naive.

"Gotcha."

I never thought that the Gannett reporter's political ideology would bias his reporting.

And even today, I am having difficulty understanding how anyone who proudly espouses liberalism could conduct himself in this manner. I see nothing "liberal" about deliberately misstating the facts with the justification that perspective matters more than accuracy. I see nothing liberal about the blatant disregard for my reputation and family.

And I see nothing liberal about the calloused disregard for

individual liberties.

(7) ALTHOUGH THE CONSTITUTION GRANTS THE PRESS THE OBLIGATION TO USE NEWSPAPERS AS A PROTECTOR OF INDIVIDUAL LIBERTIES, IT ALSO GRANTS THE PRESS A LEGAL LOOPHOLE TO USE NEWSPAPERS AS A WEAPON AGAINST INDIVIDUAL LIBERTIES.

The Courier-Journal is the only statewide newspaper in the state of Kentucky. Prior to 1986, the Courier-Journal was owned by the Bingham family. Under the Binghams, the Louisville newspaper was known for editorial positions on such important issues such as racial integration. News reporting was emphasized; profits were de-emphasized.

Included in Allen J. Share's 1993 article "A Historian's View," he stated,

> "Barry Bingham Sr. was always very conscious of the newspaper's monopoly status in the community, at one point declaring that 'the greater the power the individual exerts, the heavier is the burden on his conscience.' Bingham sought to insure openness to criti-

cism by appointing an ombudsman to the staff of The Courier-Journal in 1967, the first such position in a major American newspaper, and by maintaining what he termed a "very open" letters to the editor column..."

Barry Bingham Sr. began a policy of instituting ethical guidelines for the newspaper which his successor, Barry Bingham Jr., strengthened and expanded. In 1974, David P. Garino, writing on the front page of the Wall Street Journal, concluded that 'the Bingham papers are the acknowledged Messrs. Clean of the newspaper industry. This is no small distinction at a time when the ethics and credibility of the American press are undergoing their closest scrutiny in recent memory...'

The Courier-Journal also maintained its national ranking and its high esteem among its peers and among professors of journalism. In 1983, a Media Research Institute survey of publishers, editors and journalism professors placed The Courier-Journal among the nation's top 15 daily newspapers...

Like his father and his grandfather, Barry Bingham Jr., viewed the Courier-Journal as a public trust and was more concerned with public service than with the generation of revenue. A Wall Street Journal reporter wrote in July 1974 'the relatively low profit margin results from continually pumping revenues back into the news and editorial functions."

Tifft and Jones declared in their 1991 book,

'The Patriarch,' that Barry Bingham Jr.,'
vowed to set the pace for the rest of the
newspaper industry (in the area of journalistic
ethics), establishing higher standards of right
and wrong than ever before. This was to be
his greatest legacy...

In 1986, the Gannett Co. Inc. purchased the Courier-Journal.
Editor David V. Hawpe, who began working for the
newspaper in 1969 and was appointed editor in 1987, stated
that Gannett had left the newspaper

'with the resources necessary to do the kind of
work we've always done.''

Has the dedication to ethical journalism diminished since
corporate Gannett bought the paper, and since the influence
of the Binghams is gone?

Many doctors, such as I, have reason to think so.

The Gannett Co. is a multibillion dollar corporation with
lots of power. According to the New York Times,

"The Gannett Co. said on Oct 11, 1994 that its
third-quarter net income rose 19% to $105.5
million, compared with $88.8 million a year
earlier."

But in addition to the enormous monetary power by this
corporate giant, Gannett also has the special constitutional
power granted by the First Amendment. Thus, the Gannett
Corporation could be said to have the best of all worlds.

Compared to regular folks, Gannett has absolute power.

And some say that if power corrupts, absolute power

corrupts absolutely.

At least against doctors, the examples of investigative journalism cited in this book hardly maintain the high standard of ethics set by the Binghams.

But why has the Gannett Courier-Journal elected to act in such a tabloid manner?

Is it because the Gannett editors simply don't like doctors? Is it related to the Gannett corporate take-over in 1987? Or has the Gannett Courier-Journal simply turned away from the ethical foundation established by the Binghams?

It might be illustrative to look at other examples in which Gannett sacrificed individual liberties simply to sell newspapers, or at least to appease the vitriol of the editors.

For example, I am no advocate of the tobacco industry. In speaking with my patients, one would quickly discover that I am one of the most relentless physicians with regard to advising, begging, and pleading that my patients stop cigarette smoking - the most preventable health risk factor in the United States.

The Gannett Courier-Journal shares this outrage. But while as I have concentrated my efforts on the users, Gannett has focused much of their efforts on the source - the tobacco industry and Brown & Williamson. As a result, some friction has occurred between these two corporate giants.

After the Gannett Courier-Journal began to attack the tobacco industry with a series of reports, Brown and Williamson hit the Gannett Courier-Journal with a law suit concerning stolen documents in the possession of Gannett. As the result of this legal battle, and as the result of Gannett's role as the cigarette police, Gannett and Brown & Williamson didn't play well together.

They didn't play well together at all.

So after the law suit was filed, how did Gannett respond to Brown & Williamson' law suit? Gannett had two options. On the one hand, they could have taken the honorable approach and accepted Brown & Williamson' constitutional right to challenge their "freedom of the press," with the confidence that they, as the press, would be absolved of any wrongdoing. After all, they probably felt they were fulfilling their constitutional obligation to protect individual liberties.

On the other hand, they could take the sleazy approach and use the constitutional privilege of "freedom of the press" as a legal loophole to use newspapers as a weapon against individual liberties.

Which path do you suppose they chose?

Need I ask?

On June 19, 1994 (two weeks after the significantly fabricated, wrongful article condemning me), the front page, headline story of the day, slapped across the entire length of the paper, was the startling revelation:

> "B & W CHAIRMAN LITTLE-KNOWN,
> AND LIKES IT THAT WAY"

I am not kidding.

This was the real, unabridged headline.

Unbelievable.

Was this a breaking story of national or regional importance? Was this the death of a President? Was this a breakout of war? Or was this simply a chance to use the newspaper for character assassination?

To answer this perplexing question, it is illuminating to see the focus of the article. Among the important, front page, lead-headline things we learned was:

> "He has been lampooned in Doonesbury as a member of the "Carcinogen Seven.""...

> As an industry leader, he's been virtually invisible...

> Before this spring, his picture had been published only once in 12 years in this newspaper - ... where he toiled mostly in the background as a fund-raiser for a handful of civic causes. Center stage is not his favorite place...

> Former employees at every level say he is ... better known as a brutally demanding and volatile executive who is legendary for shouting and swearing at subordinates...

> The vast majority of employees are scared to death of the man, said Brian Stauss, a former client systems manager. "I have never seen the man exhibit compassion.."

So what was the purpose of this article, particularly as the front page, lead headline article of the day? If the purpose

The Courier – Journal

B & W chairman little-known, and likes it that way

By ANDREW WOLFSON
Staff Writers

He has been lampooned in Doonesbury as a member of the "Carcinogen Seven.

Nelson County's most profound sorrow

Members of a National Guard artillery posed for photo during Vietnam war

Community remembers Vietnam's terrible toll

SECOND STORY

Directly below the front page, lead headline story of the day was the article "Nelson County's most profound sorrow." In the 1950's, Vietnam became embroiled in a civil war. The United States gave its support to South Vietnamese President Ngo Kinh Diem over the communist Ho Chi Minh and the Viet Cong. Due to the fear of spreading communism, the United States sent troops to assist South Vietnam - escalating year after painful year to a peak of over 500,000 U.S. troops The drafting of young men to fight and die in this conflict resulted in one of the most turbulent, and painful times in American history. The domestic unrest that ensued continues to have ramifications today. This story described how young Nelson County men went to war, vowing to their families that they would return. On a June evening, "five members of a Bardstown-based Kentucky National Guard artillery battery died or were fatally injured at a place called Fire Base Tomahawk."

FRONT PAGE, LEAD HEADLINE STORY OF THE DAY

The lead story "B & W chairman little-known, and likes it that way" described how this corporate head of a tobacco company had employees who thought he was a jerk. Less than a year later, he would resign due to the potential fatal blood disease known as aplastic anemia.

QUESTIONS

The headline of this story indicates that the B & W chairman enjoyed his privacy. It is in the Ninth Amendment wherein the Supreme Court has denoted citizens' "right to privacy." Is it a violation of the "right to privacy" to report a front page story about how a citizen likes his privacy?

Why is the quoting of employees who thought this man was a jerk of greater journalistic merit than the death of the young Kentucky men who served in the Vietnam war?

was to report that the Brown and Williamson Chairman was a citizen who liked his privacy, then why would Gannett deny his "right to privacy" with this front page story? If the purpose was to expose the chairman as committing illegal acts that warranted front page news, then why did they focus on quoting disgruntled employees who tried to make him look like a jerk.

I suspect that the real purpose was two-fold. First of all, Gannett simply didn't like the man. Hence, the man must pay. Secondly, this was a message. It was a message to anyone else who considered challenging Gannett. It was a message that any challenge to Gannett would result in retribution of the greatest magnitude, even if it meant dismantling a few individual liberties along the way.

On April 22, 1995, less than one year later, it was reported that this chairman resigned. He did not resign due to the efforts of Gannett to discredit him. He resigned because he had developed a rare blood disease known as aplastic anemia.

Was it worth it Gannett? Do you feel vindicated?

I share the Gannett Courier-Journal's bias that cigarette smoking should be discouraged. But even with my strongest of biases, I do not believe it serves any cause to use the front page of the only state-wide newspaper in Kentucky, simply to ridicule those with whom I disagree. Using the front page simply to make someone look like a jerk is a sinister abuse of the privilege of the First Amendment.

But even more sinister was the implicit statement to anyone

else who dared challenge the mighty Gannett - one of the select corporations in America with absolute power. The statement to anyone who considered challenging wrongdoings of Gannett was made loud and clear.

Do not question, and do not mess with Gannett.

But if by chance I had missed this article, or had simply not been paying attention, this message was reaffirmed in a threat to me by the Gannett Corporate attorney.

After I had gone through every means possible to achieve justice for the wrongful acts against my reputation and family as the result of an irresponsible press, I contacted the ombudsman in one last plea for help in order to *avoid* litigation. (Please recall that the Binghams had established the ombudsman precisely for this purpose.) But rather than a response from the ombudsman, I received a letter from the Gannett Corporate attorney who, in his letter of 10/27, 1995, stated,

> "I hope that you will reconsider the idea of litigation. It will serve no purpose, but will only further publicize the essential facts of the story which you apparently find distasteful. I must also advise you that The Courier-Journal is committed to fully defend itself in all such cases. Such a defense will include an effort to recover all its costs and legal fees from you after the case has been dismissed."

I must say, being from southern Kentucky, I have a low threshold for threats.

Subsequently, I sought legal counsel. After brief negotiations with my attorney, the mighty Gannett immediately agreed to a letter of apology in a legal settlement.

In retrospect, although I was successful in achieving some important goals, it was only after extraordinary effort, persistence, and expense. And the fact that Gannett has yet to publicly apologize still brings to question whether or not justice was fully served.

So again, who is at fault? Has the deterioration in the ethical standards of the Gannett Courier-Journal occurred due to the buy-out by Gannett? Or has the deterioration in the ethical standards occurred due to the loss of the influence of the Binghams and others who treasured, above all else, truth? This is not a trivial question.

If it is true that state-wide newspapers bought by corporate giants are subject to loss of journalistic ethics, then such buy-outs of monopolistic newspapers should be reconsidered in the future. But if it is true that the loss of journalistic ethics are due to the emergence of post-Bingham reporters and editors who have forsaken the basic journalistic standards of truth and fairness, then perhaps the time has come for Gannett to assume a more active oversight role.

Either way, unethical conduct of the press is not acceptable. It violates the trust our founding fathers had in an institution who was granted the privilege to help protect individual liberties and to serve the public good.

And it is difficult to see how the press can be expected to fulfill their constitutional obligation to protect individual liberties if they continue to be granted the constitutional loophole to use newspapers as a weapon against individual liberties.

(8) APOLOGY AND ATONEMENT FOR WRONGDOING IS ETHICALLY REQUIRED ONLY OF THOSE ON THE OTHER SIDE OF THE FIRST AMENDMENT.

No one is more indignant about preaching ethics than the editors of the Gannett Courier-Journal. Not just ethical behavior, but also the *appearance* of ethical behavior is routinely expected of government officials, as well as corporate leaders. And if a Kentucky Congressman, or if a Kentucky corporate leader is found to have acted in an unethical or irresponsible manner, you can bet that their names and faces will grace the front pages without reservation.

Because ethics and ethical behavior is a big deal.

And Gannett knows ethics.

For example, although I know next to nothing about the status of newspaper journalists, it seems to me that David Hawpe, lead editor of the Gannett Courier-Journal since 1987, is a also a big deal. According to the Jefferson Medical Society News, February/March 1995,

"Hawpe has served as C-J editor since 1987...

Hawpe is a graduate of Louisville Male High School and the University of Kentucky. He completed a Standford University summer program in media law and a Harvard University Nieman Fellowship. He has taught at Harvard University, University of Louisville and University of Kentucky and is a frequent lecturer at the Poynter Institute of writing ethics and management. He serves as a lecturer on writing and newsroom management for the American Press Institute and has been a Pulitzer juror four times.

Hawpe has served on the Board of Directors of the Associated Press Managing Editors, the APME Foundation, and he was president of the Kentucky Press Association Board of Directors. He has chaired several committees for the American Society of Newspaper Editors.

A proponent of journalism education, Hawpe has served on the advisory committees of [numerous universities].

He chairs the university of North Carolina at Chapel Hill School of Journalism School of Visitors and serves on the Accreditation Committee of the Accrediting Council on Journalism and Mass Communications..."

Mr. Hawpe clearly represents a main-stream, respected, 90's newspaper editor. He has trained and taught at Harvard. Furthermore, he is a "frequent lecturer" on "writing and ethics."

This needs to be emphasized. David Hawpe, the lead editor

of a Gannett Newspaper is not just considered an ethical person, not just an ethical journalist, but he is also considered to have demonstrated such journalistic ethical conduct as to have other journalists look to him as they try to learn to become more ethical in their own reporting.

So the questions are obvious.

What is there about being a doctor that would prompt this respected teacher of journalistic ethics to allow unfair and inaccurate trashing of doctors' reputations?

Is not fairness a good lesson in teaching ethics in journalism?

After our face-to-face meeting, in which he gave me his word that someone would inquire as to my efforts with the homeless and to my medical research to help me regain some of my reputation wrongfully lost, why did he not keep his word?

Is not keeping your word a good lesson in teaching ethics in journalism?

And why had this champion of journalistic morality declined atonement for blatant lies reported in his own newspaper?

Is not truth a good lesson in teaching ethics in journalism?

Which brings to mind another curious phenomenon of the press. I have learned that editors have a strange notion of atonement. Whenever I met with the editors, I had the distinct impression that they felt a face-to-face meeting alone, without subsequent action, was sufficient to atone for any wrong committed.

I also learned that these meetings serve another curious purpose that works to the advantage of reporters and editors. I have learned that journalists often view meetings with the wrongfully accused after the story has been reported as an educational experience. In one sense, it is reassuring that some journalists take an interest in the positions of the accused. But in another sense, why is it necessary to wait until *after* the story is written to get the whole story?

It seems to me that the answer lies in the fact that editors feel that many investigative stories are good "on the job training" for their inexperienced reporters. Basically, a reporter, who may have no clue, or only a peripheral clue of the subject matter being investigated, is set out to find a "real person" to create a particular perspective. A deadline is given.

The clock is started.

The rush is on.

Being that the reporter sometimes has little understanding of what is sometimes very complex issues, and being that the reporter has even less time to adequately research the very complex issues, the reporter is often required to take the easy way out. And the easy way out is to base the story, not on facts, but on the reporter's concept of what's going on. Or, the reporter may simply create a story that realizes the perspective of his editors. And for those innocent people whose reputations get trashed along the way, they can always have a face-to-face meeting with the editors and reporters, after the story has been reported.

But while as I appreciate how this may work to the advantage of editors and reporter, it is hardly ethical.

Finally, I have learned that the press views themselves as somehow courageous when they boldly state "We stand behind our story," or "We fully support our reporter." But this willingness to support even the most incompetent reporter is not based on courage. Instead, it is based on the fact that the First Amendment of the Constitution virtually guarantees the press will win any legal argument.

And again, while I appreciate how the abuse of the "freedom of the press" may work to the advantage of editors and reporters, it is hardly ethical.

In my view, the "freedom of the press" denotes a supreme obligation, rather than simply a legal device to avoid litigation. And while the press is very fond of referring to the "Freedom of the Press" clause of the First Amendment, I might also suggest referral to the "Do unto others..." clause of the Bible, and/or the "What's Good for the Goose..." clause of common sense.

My point is, I challenge the Gannett Courier-Journal reporters and editors to apply their own standard of atonement to others. I challenge Gannett to agree to drop any future investigative report against a rogue employee of a corporation, or a corrupt government official as long as a corporate or governmental official agrees to simply meet with the reporter and the injured party. And if the corporate or governmental officials courageously states: "We stand behind our actions," I challenge the Gannett Courier-Journal to praise them for their courageousness.

But I doubt those in the press would accept this challenge, because it appears that apology and atonement for wrongdoing is ethically required only of those on the other side of the First Amendment.

====================

(9) EXPOSING THE WRONGDOINGS AND UNETHICAL BEHAVIOR OF THE COR- PORATIONS AND GOVERNMENT OFFICIALS IS A CONSTITUTIONAL OBLIGATION; EXPOSING THE WRONG- DOINGS AND UNETHICAL BEHAVIOR OF THE CORPORATE PRESS IS INAPPRO- PRIATE.

I had worked and lived all across the Commonwealth of Kentucky. Furthermore, I have family in southern Kentucky. Because the Gannett Courier-Journal is the only statewide newspaper in Kentucky, the significantly fabricated, front page, lead headline story was big news to my friends and family. Even as long as six months, it was clearly on the minds of many.

For example, during the Christmas holidays, most families begin conversation of yuletide visits. Other families talk of gifts. Some other families might even talk of Christ. But my first conversation with my father (who lives in Southern Kentucky) during the Christmas season began with:

"Hey dad, how's it goin?"' I said.

164

> "Oh not to bad. How's it going with you? I guess you must not be doing too bad because we haven't read anything about you in the paper recently."

So point is, if there is anyone who thinks that a significantly fabricated, front page, lead headline story with the accusation of overcharging patients doesn't dramatically effect one's family and reputation, then they simply don't know what they're talking about.

And I think my letter to the Vice President and Lead Editor is worth repeating:

> "My Mother, who is paralyzed in the legs due to a damaged cervical disc, was first presented with this article, during a rehabilitation outpatient visit, when the nurses...showed her the article about how her son was a criminal. My colleagues who know me are sympathetic to my position and are outraged at the Courier-Journal. My colleagues who don't know me are uncertain. My practice has suffered. My family and practice have been wrongfully harmed."

To right this wrong, I requested a public apology from Gannett. However, through my attorney, I was told that Gannett would not agree to such apology because,

> "You can't expect to tell the press what to print."

Nevertheless, I was determined to clear my name. Because I thought injustice by the corporate press was every bit as newsworthy as injustice by corporations, I wrote my hometown newspaper - the "Park City Daily News." I had hoped that they would at least help me clear my name with my family and friends back home.

But they responded that any reporting of this matter was,

"Inappropriate."

I am not kidding.

Unbelievable.

Inappropriate?

They did not say that it was boring. They did not say it was uninteresting. They did not say it was unimportant. They didn't even say that I was wrong. But instead, they felt that any reporting against corporate Gannett, even with documentation of an admission of guilt was "inappropriate."

I have thought long and hard as to why my hometown newspaper had forsaken me, and had felt that reporting the injustice against me was "inappropriate."

Perhaps they thought that while as corporate injustice is front page news, *press* injustice is no news.

Perhaps they felt that *any* criticism of the press is inappropriate, regardless of the atrocity. (And you can bet that many of those in the press reading this book will simply write it off as "press bashing." These people don't have a clue as to what it is like living on this side of the First Amendment).

Or perhaps they were scared of Gannett. I can certainly sympathize. It is conceivable that Gannett holds so much power, that it would be financially foolish for a smaller newspaper to challenge this multibillion dollar giant. It would be most ironic if the very freedoms that were intended to protect individual liberties, also served to protect the multibillion dollar corporate press as they dismantle individual liberties.

Either way, I am struck by the hypocrisy. As a doctor, I have heard countless criticism as to why "all doctors stick together." In fact, it is probably true that at times, doctors have been too cautious in reporting colleagues who they suspect no longer meet the high ethical or professional standard of the medical profession. Nonetheless, I receive regular notifications of numerous doctors - including names and addresses - who are sanctioned by the Kentucky Medical Revue Board. In these notifications, the loss of privileges and even loss of licenses of numerous doctor colleagues is listed.

Some of the doctors so sanctioned are even reported in the newspapers.

But although sanctioning fellow colleagues is unpleasant, it is, nevertheless, proper. So how would newspaper editors feel if doctors suddenly decided to stop pursuing abuses and wrongful acts among fellow doctors? What would editors think of doctors who fail to atone for uncaring, deliberate acts that result in unwarranted injury to their patients? How abusive would editors perceive the medical profession if the First Amendment included a "freedom of the medicine" provision that essentially abolished malpractice.

You can bet the editorials would be flying. Why, the newspaper editors might even think the medical profession as out-of-touch, elitist, and arrogant.

But what about reporting specific unethical or unprofessional behavior of the press? Why is exposing the wrongdoings and unethical behavior of corporations, government officials and doctors a constitutional obligation, while as exposing the wrongdoings and unethical behavior of the corporate press "inappropriate?"

(10) JOURNALISM IS NO LONGER A PROFESSION.

What is a profession?

> Profession: n., a vocation or occupation requiring advanced education and training and involving intellectual skills, as medicine, law, theology, engineering, teaching, etc.

But in addition, most folks believe that true professions require a high level of ethical conduct. That is why so many professions have oaths and such. For example, in medicine, we have the Hippocratic oath. This is an example of an ethical goal. The original version of this oath was:

> "I swear by Apollo Physician and Asclepius and Hygieia and Panaccia and all the gods and goddesses, making them my witnesses, that I will fulfill according to my ability and judgment this oath and this covenant:

> To hold him who has taught me this as equal to my parents and to live my life in partnership with him, and if he is in need of money to give him a share of mine, and to regard his offspring as equal to my brothers in male lineage and to teach them this art - if they desire to learn it - without fee and

covenant; to give a share of precepts and oral instructions and all the other learning to my sons and to the sons of him who has instructed me and to pupils who have signed the covenant and have taken an oath according to the medical law, but to no one else.

I will apply dietetic measures for the benefit of the sick according to my ability and judgment; I will keep them from harm and injustice.

I will neither give a deadly drug to anybody if asked for it, nor will I make a suggestion to this effect. Similarly I will not give to a woman an abortive remedy. In purity and holiness I will guard my life and my art.

I will not use the knife, not even on sufferers from stone, but will withdraw in favor of such men as are engaged in this work.

Whatever houses I may visit, I will come for the benefit of the sick, remaining free of all intentional injustice, of all mischief and in particular of sexual relations with both female and male persons, be they free or slaves.

What I may see or hear in the course of the treatment or even outside of the treatment in regard to the life of men, which on no account one must spread abroad, I will keep to myself holding such things shameful to be spoken about.

If I fulfill this oath and do not violate it, may it be granted to me to enjoy life and art, being honored with fame among all men for all time

to come; if I transgress it and swear falsely,
may the opposite of this be my lot"

From a practical standpoint, few physicians today spend a lot of time swearing to Apollo, Asclepius, Hygieia, and Panaceia. We typically don't give money to our medical school teachers. And most of us don't make a lot of house calls. However, although we no longer strictly adhere to the Hippocratic oath, most all physicians strongly adhere to the Hippocratic principle of,

"primum non nocere."

This translates into,

"First, do no harm."

This simple principle is among the most profound directives in all of medicine. As a physician, we must always insure that before any treatment is instituted, that regardless of the perceived or theoretical benefit, no treatment should be recommended if it is likely to cause unwarranted harm. By applying this simple principle, numerous lives have been saved, and countless patients have avoided harm. It is the most basic ethical standard of medicine.

But what constitutes ethics in journalism?

Would not "primum non nocere" also be a reasonable principle for journalists? Should we not expect reporters and editors to be sure that before any story is published, that regardless of the perceived benefit, no story should be published if it causes unwarranted harm to the individual liberties of citizens?

And above this, is it not reasonable to assume that it is the dedication to protecting individual liberties through reporting the truth that defines journalism as a profession? These, in my judgement, are the minimal standards for ethical journalism.

But obviously this is not a universal standard.

This is not to say that unethical journalism is always the result of unethical journalists. In my judgment, many editors have good intentions. But because of institutional influences that occur whenever isolation from the general public occurs, sometimes editors simply lose touch with how their actions directly contradict their principles.

They just forget that it is action, not intention, that makes us what we are.

For example, David Hawpe, the lead editor and vice president at the Gannett Courier-Journal wrote an article about "hyper-journalism" in 1993. Selected portions of this article included:

> HYPER-JOURNALISM VS. THE PUBLIC INTEREST
>
> February 21, 1993
>
> "...Readers and viewers deserve better than this.
>
> Some editors think it's all right to rush into a public controversy at the last minute...and publish the most outrageous examples of abuse they can find. They jubilantly announce they have exposed another public crisis, and

demand adoption of the most extreme solutions.

Meanwhile, somebody in a back room is working up a reprint to submit for one of those ubiquitous journalism prizes. Indeed, it's so bad that the prize reprints almost beat the original stories off the press.

This is the journalism of exploitation, the strategy for which is simple, and simplistic.

Generate public anger and, as a result, public support for some kind of change.

Public understanding of the issue? Forget it. Finesse in dealing with issues? Nothing but a sellout. Tolerance for negotiation and tradeoff? The last refuge of the corrupted. Or so they would have you believe.

The folks who do this kind of journalism don't seem to worry when the public dialogue becomes an exercise in puffery and exhortation.

There is always time, they argue, for decision-makers to moderate the passions that are stirred by hyper-journalism. Our system ensures (they say, with a knowing smile) that any strong public policy brew will be diluted with the milk of compromise...

It's easy to claim that you are raising a strong populist voice in the public dialogue, as long as you measure it only by the decibel level. It's easy to dismiss your critics as too close to the system, too protective of the ... existing institutions. That avoids any uncomfortable discussions about the value of rigor and discipline, as opposed to boldness and confrontation...

It is destructive to indulge in unfair, broad-brush criticism of society's basic institutions. Such tactics can turn support for reform into alienation...

Hyper-journalism ruins the public dialogue. It discourages precision in our readers' under-standing of public, and private institutions. It provokes a greater loss of confidence in those institutions than may be warranted by events and circumstances. It creates a constituency for ham-fisted, counter-productive remedies, not for wise reforms...

If journalists approach each new topic the same way - if each new subject is a crisis, reverberating with the same sound and fury - then readers and viewers won't know the difference between big issues and little ones. What's more, they will be tempted to believe that nothing good is happening in the public realm, which isn't the case.

Most public problems are complicated. Few will respond to simple solutions. Real answers usually requires some mediation and mode-ration.

It's tough enough to build a constituency for that kind of temperance, without hyper-journalists whipping the crowd into a frenzy.

Some pencil-wielding, career-carrying block-heads are determined to follow their misplaced enthusiasms out the window...

That kind of journalism desensitizes the public. It trivializes the whole roster of public concerns. It needlessly undercuts citizen confidence in our system's methods and mechanisms...

This is not a Kentucky problem, this is a national dilemma.

We see it every evening on TV, as the Brit Humes of the world give you their breathless nightly assessments of the barely born Clinton administration...

As Barry Bingham Sr., long the editor and publisher of The Courier-Journal, warned in 1970, the excesses of the media can lead to their own undoing. He said, "A loss of confidence in the press is one of the factors that contributes to public frustration. If it goes far enough, it can convince many people that the protection of a free press is no longer in their interest and therefore expendable."

Some editors encourage apocalyptic journalism because they want to win prizes, an that's a shame.

Some writers indulge in it because they don't want to be called chicken. They don't seem at all embarrassed by the fact that they sound just like Chicken Little.

The balance of the article went on to criticize the Lexington Herald, a Lexington Ky. newspaper, because it had supposedly been guilty of "hyper-journalism" in its editorials of an ethics bill passed by the Ky. legislature.

But in a more general standpoint, David Hawpe is clearly passionate in his criticism of those "other" journalists who conduct themselves in "hyper-journalism."

Fast forward to 1994, and note what he did to me, my reputation, and my family.

(I wonder how soon the "prize reprints" were sent after the significantly fabricated, front page, lead article was reported against me).

I think that a huge gap exists between how editors view themselves, and how they act. Although he may not recognize it, I believe that David Hawpe is no less capable of "hyper-journalism" than his colleagues.

This contradiction may be as the result of many factors.

First of all, editors such as David Hawpe have become very comfortably assimilated into high paying jobs with the corporate press. As such, perhaps their passion for protecting the individual liberties of citizens has been replaced by corporate concerns.

Secondly, editors live in a surreal environment of the press with the great wall of the First Amendment that divides them from the rest of us folks.

They have no real obligation to insist on fairness and accuracy. They are the press.

They have no real obligation to atone for wrongful acts.

They are the press.

They have no real mechanism to ensure accountability and responsibility. They are the press.

They have no binding obligation to fulfill their constitutional obligation to protect individual liberties. They are the press.

They have become part of the Corporate press industry.

They have become comfortably numb.

They have become part of the problem.

And as such, they have forgotten that, above all else, it is the dedication to protecting individual liberties through reporting the truth that defines journalism as a profession.

THE PERSPECTIVE

CHAPTER 4: THIS CAN'T BE HAPPENING TO AMERICANS

"Business and government are not allowed to act solely on the basis of primordial urges. Reasonable restraints exist in our judicial system to harness these acts. However, the press has been given constitutional protection to act on their primordial urges, often without reasonable restraints."

THE TEN RULES OF 90' JOURNALISM

Thus far, the discussion of the "Ten Rules of 90's Journalism" has been limited to my own, personal experiences. But do these same rules apply to the press at large?

I think most folks would agree they do.

But why does the press act in such a destructive manner?

Simply put, negative stories are less risky and less work-intensive than positive, constructive stories. In his article, "The Media's Message - The Public Thinks the National Press is Elitist, Insensitive and Arrogant" (U.S. News, January 9, 1995), Stephen Budiansky quotes an ABC reporter as been quoted as saying,

> "You can be wrong, as long as you're negative and skeptical. But if you're going to say something remotely positive, you'd better be 150 percent right or you're going to be accused of rolling over."

Stephen Budiansky also reports Marvin Kalb, a former NBC reporter who is now at Harvard University's John F.

Kennedy School of Government as saying,

> "There is a mean-spiritedness to American
> journalism, a desire to tear down rather than
> build up. You cannot be positive today. You
> cannot even give a public official the benefit
> of the doubt."

The reason that negative, destructive stories are easier than positive, constructive stories is at least partially due to the cynicism that has been created when dealing with politicians. The use of the "spin" has destroyed much of the trust between the politicians and the press.

"Spin" is a term that originally described efforts of a politician or political party to highlight the best aspects of a particular issue. Unfortunately, in recent years, "spin" has turned into nothing less than intentional deception to gain political advantage. According to Stephen Budiansky, Joe Peyronnin, vice president of CBS news has said,

> "They'll look you straight in the eye and tell
> you things they don't believe. You just can't
> take anything at face value."

So it has become incumbent on reporters to be skeptical of virtually anything they are told in order to avoid being duped.

And it doesn't take too many face-to-face lies for skepticism to evolve into cynicism.

Believe me, I know.

And if any positive "spin" is to be reported, it must only occur after painstaking evaluation of all the facts from all sides of the issue. Hence, in an environment where a story is required to be written and published within a set deadline, sometimes within hours of an event, the reporter simply doesn't have the time to examine all the facts necessary to print a positive story.

And beyond that, positive stories about politicians or governmental policy rarely receives accolades from fellow journalists. I doubt there are many who have won journalistic admiration by steadfastly supporting positive contributions of the establishment.

On the other hand, negative criticism is a applauded, and is a lot easier. Anyone can criticize. I once heard Senator Phil Gramm say,

> "It takes a carpenter to build a barn. It only
> takes a mule to kick it down.

Negative criticism is easy because it often requires only an opinion, and doesn't necessary require the messy and time-consuming work of researching, or understanding the facts. Again, according to Stephen Budiansky, Hal Bruno of ABC (American Broadcasting Company) has said,

> "There is a lack of discipline, a laziness. I
> don't think everyone has to wear the hair
> shirt I did. But those years I spent on the
> police beat, I learned a lot about people and a
> lot about myself. One thing you learn is that
> when you're cynical you lose touch with
> things."

And as long as journalists have absolute power, this "laziness" will continue to harm innocent human lives.

(1) PERSPECTIVE MATTERS MORE THAN ACCURACY.

The journalistic axiom that perspective matters more than accuracy is a revisitation of the often debated "does the ends justify the means?" Some would argue that extreme circumstances sometimes warrant extreme "by any means necessary" directives. But I do not believe it serves the press' best interest, much less the citizen's best interest to make this a universal journalistic law.

Because it seems to me that it is the dedication to protecting individual liberties through reporting the truth that defines journalism as a profession.

But numerous examples exist where perspective is given priority over accuracy.

On November 16, 1992, on their "Dateline" program, NBC (National Broadcasting System) telecast a "gotcha" story concerning General Motor's (GMC) trucks. Due to allegations of safety problems with the placement of the fuel tanks, it was NBC's "perspective" that GMC pickup trucks routinely exploded when being hit. So NBC began to ram trucks into each other on camera. But apparently, they were having a hard time getting the trucks to explode.

And this *should* have been the real story.

But instead, NBC felt that the "perspective" of the story outweighed the facts of the story. So to create the proper "perspective," devices were used by remote control to ignite the trucks during the filmed crash tests.

They achieved their perspective.

The trucks exploded.

So, since it appears that "perspective over accuracy" is regarded, at least by some in the press, to be an important axiom in reporting the news, I would like to note two objections to this concept. My first objective is procedural. My second is ethical.

THE SCIENTIFIC METHOD

From a procedural standpoint, perspective over accuracy may result in gross scientific error. As a doctor and researcher, my knowledge and training is based on the scientific method. The scientific method involves making a hypothesis, followed by unbiased, objective testing to prove, or disprove the hypothesis. This method of medical research has been the driving force behind the incredible advancements in understanding, and treating disease. Because the unbiased truth is so vital towards achieving real answers, meticulous efforts are made to ensure that all research, and all researchers, adhere to the principles of the scientific method.

For example, when evaluating the efficacy and safety of new drugs, the drug being tested is often compared to a placebo (a sugar pill). If the drug has been shown in animals to be dramatically effective and remarkably safe, it would be tempting to develop a "perspective" that it would have the same effectiveness and safety in humans. This "perspective" might bias the opinions of the researchers and/or patients. And biased researchers and/or patients might confound and skew the results of subsequent studies.

Therefore, it is the standard of practice in research to expect clinical trials to be "double-blinded." The term "double-blind" means that neither the patient, nor the doctor knows whether the patient is receiving study drug or placebo.

The recognition of the need to eliminate bias in medical research is so great that studies require the placebo to be identical in shape, color, and form as the study drug. Furthermore, the placebo must be taken at the same time as the study drug. All these meticulous efforts are made for the sole purpose of eliminating bias, and to facilitate finding the real truth. Finally, even after all these efforts, any positive findings must be repeated in many other such unbiased clinical trials before consideration of approval of the study drug.

As a result of such efforts, truthful and reliable information is obtained. And the ability to rely on these scientifically derived truths has spurned an explosion in the progress of understanding and treating disease. But as importantly, these unbiased studies have revealed countless treatments that turned out to be useless, or even harmful. Despite the sometimes overwhelming theoretical benefits, and despite the hopes of the most well-meaning researchers, countless treatments have been kept off the market due to unintended, harmful side effects. In fact, some promising treatments have been found to worsen the very disease they were meant to cure - all because of the result of the scientific method.

Hence, we in medicine can tolerate no breeches in the unbiased pursuit of the truth. And it is the relentless pursuit of truth that not only has been responsible for constructive achievement, but also responsible for the avoidance of destructive harm to human lives.

I think the same should hold true for reporting. Those reporters who feel their perspective is somehow above accuracy engage in a critical procedural error. And as such, they run the risk of being responsible for demeaning constructive achievement, and being responsible for propagating unwarranted and preventable harm to human lives.

ETHICS

"The ends justify the means."

Many journalists believe that as long as the ends is well-intentioned, the manner by which the goal is reached is not relevant. But history is replete with examples of wrongful acts that were justified to the public on the grounds of reaching a well-intentioned endpoint. Spain had inquisitions in the 1400's against those accused of heresy. Nazi Germany had concentration camps in the 1940's to ethnically "cleanse" their society.

And in American history we had the Salem witch trials.

In 1692, two young daughters of the Reverend Samuel Parris were diagnosed as being under the spell of a witch. The girls (accusers) then picked out spell-casting "witches" in the community who were subsequently seized and put on trial. This precipitated an outbreak of witch citings with more than 140 people accused of witchcraft in 1692 alone. As time went on, the definition of being a witch began to include anyone offensive to the Reverend Parris.

The first session of the court to try these witches had a docket of more than 70 cases.

26 were convicted, and 19 were executed.

Had he been asked, I'm sure the well-intentioned, good reverend would have agreed that the elimination of witchcraft certainly justified the executions of human lives. But today, I think most people feel that witch hunts probably should be disbanded.

And this is not to say that the unbridled vigilantism practiced against doctors by Gannett compares in severity to the Spanish Inquisition, Nazi concentration camps, or the Salem execution of witches. However, this *is* to say that the ends doesn't necessarily always justify the means. And it would seem that from a moral standpoint, the means in researching and reporting a story should be based on fact - not on the perceived, predetermined perspective.

Because it is the dedication to protecting individual liberties through reporting the truth that defines journalism as a profession.

(2) CITIZENS ACCUSED OF WRONGDO-ING ARE PRESUMED FRONT PAGE GUILTY UNTIL PROVEN BACK PAGE INNOCENT.

As of the writing of this book, President Bill Clinton's approval rating was not as high as it could be. He had been personally responsible for much of the criticism against him. Nevertheless, part of his poor approval rating had at least partially been due to unfair treatment by the press.

For example, in 1993, the national press reported that an unnamed Federal Aviation Administration spokesman in Los Angeles had stated that two commuter flights were delayed due to a Hollywood hairstyling received by the President. The President of the United States was portrayed to the public as elitist, as someone who feels his haircut was worth more than the time of the public he was sworn to serve.

However, in reality, no such delay took place. But how many newspapers, and how many in the media spent as much time and as much news space correcting the error as reporting the error?

Not many.

Why?

President Clinton also was routinely hammered by the Republican party and a willing press regarding possible campaign fund rules violations involving an Arkansas investment known as Whitewater development. As of the time of this writing, the President had not as yet been directly implicated in any miscarriage of justice. Nevertheless, he has been pummeled by many in the press for things that "might" have occurred.

I do not know what the outcome of all the Whitewater investigations will be, but I will make a prediction. If President Clinton is found innocent of all charges and innuendos, I will predict that the press will not - I repeat - will not spend one tenth the time in reporting his innocence as they did in their accusations and implications of guilt.

Why?

And what can be said about the conduct of the Democratic party and the press with regard to the trashing of House Majority Leader Newt Gingrich? Time and space does not allow even the most brief discussion of this outrage.

It is tragic that such treatment of our leaders is an accepted consequence of choosing to serve the public. Unfortunately, it is apparently understood that politicians should not only accept, but expect being publicly "roughed up" as a price for entering into public service. Why this should be so, I have no idea. But it is a sacrifice many public officials are willing to make. And, at the same time, it is also a sacrifice others, who may be better qualified, are not willing to make.

Hence, the press feels that anyone who is running for, or who is appointed to a government office should be required to undergo the journalistic equivalent of a public colonoscopy.

But while as this might be accepted practice with regard to government or public officials, it seems unreasonable and unfair to expect regular folks to be subject to the same treatment - particularly if they have done nothing wrong.

Furthermore, while as the politicians have sophisticated mechanisms to deal with an irresponsible press, the average citizen hasn't got a chance.

Because if a citizen is accused of front page guilt, and is later found to be innocent, most folks do not have the ability to use the media outlets available to the politicians and corporations. Folks who are wrongfully accused by the press usually cannot set the record straight through franking privileges, TV, radio, advertisements, etc. In fact, it is at the sole discretion of the press to decide which of the wrongfully accused are granted a reprieve, and which of the wrongfully accused are left to linger in a state of purgatory between having done nothing wrong, and being perceived of as having done something wrong.

And in an ultimate example of conflict of interest, the decision as to if, when, and where to correct wrongful accusations with the truth is left solely up to the very people who approved of the wrongful accusations in the first place.

It should, therefore, be of no surprise that those who are accused of front page guilt, often only receive a back page reprieve, if they receive any reprieve at all.

COMPARISON OF WHITEWATERGATE AND MS. DOCTOR SHOPPINGATE

	CLINTON	BAYS (me)
Current occupation	President	Doctor
Previous occupation	Governor	Janitor
Time of allegations	Years before elected President	Years before current practice
Potential fallout	Devastating to reputation and credibility	Devastating to reputation and credibility
Probability of wrong-doing from known facts	Low probability	Low probability
Perception of wrong-doing despite the facts	Very high	Very high
Time granted by the press to respond to allegations	Two years	One day
Public status	Public servant	Citizen
Counsel	Top advisors	None
Media outlets to respond	TV, radio, newspapers, etc.	Possibly a "letter to the editor" from wife
Recognized risk of unfair criticism by the press before choosing occupation	Yes	No
Others who suffer fallout of wrongful accusations	Democrats in general, Clinton's family, friends	Doctors in general, Dr. Bays' family, friends

(3) CONSTITUTIONAL LIBERTIES DO NOT APPLY DURING TRIAL BY THE PRESS.

To be tried and convicted by the press is often a far more greater punishment than being convicted by government. If the press chooses to do so, they have the power to significantly damage small and large businesses. The press has even been known to facilitate resignations or impeachment of high-level government officials. So while as corporations and government officials may have power, the press, in some respects, can be argued to have absolute power.

And it is said that if power corrupts, absolute power corrupts absolutely.

Although pockets of protest occur now and then, the power of the press has not caused widespread, organized outrage among the masses because the press has traditionally limited it's attacks to business and government. As a natural consequence, business and government have developed sophisticated techniques to deal with the press. In fact, some businesses and government officials have at times, successfully manipulated the press to their own advantage.

Furthermore, corporations and governmental officials often have alternative media (advertisement, TV, radio, etc.) available to respond.

Hence, the press and business/government have developed an antithesis relationship. They have developed a balance that both recognize. They have established a game with balanced rules.

They have established detente.

But what happens when the massive powers of the press (traditionally reserved for the equally massive powers of government/corporations) are used against regular folks. Most citizens do not have access to the defensive techniques required to defend themselves. Therefore, if the press chooses to attack citizens, most regular folks don't have a chance.

Believe me, I know.

Therefore, in my judgement, the press should be as, if not more conscious of individual liberties during trial by the press as with trial by jury.

For example, I believe the "gotcha" technique of journalism compromises justice. And during my face-to-face meeting with the lead editor and Vice President of the Gannett Courier-Journal, I brought up this very issue. I brought up the Fifth Amendment.

I brought up Miranda rights.

Ernesto Miranda was a mentally deficient man who, in 1966, was arrested for kidnapping and rape. He was not told that he had a right to an attorney, and within two hours of police questioning, confessed to kidnapping and rape.

The Supreme Court overturned the conviction. Chief Justice Earl Warren wrote:

> "Even without employing brutality...the very fact of custodial interrogation exacts a heavy toll on individual liberty and trades on the weaknesses of individuals... It is obvious that such an interrogation environment is created for no other purpose than to subjugate the individual to the will of the examiner. This atmosphere carries it's own badge of intimidation."

Since this decision, the Supreme Court no longer upholds confessions as voluntary unless the accused was advised before questioning of the following:

- (1) You have the right to remain silent
- (2) Anything you say can be used against you in court.
- (3) You have the right to an attorney and to have the attorney present while you are being questioned.
- (4) If you cannot afford an attorney, one will be appointed for you before any question begins.

After the court overturned the conviction, Miranda was retried and convicted based on other evidence. The point is, if one is truly guilty, then justice can, and in most cases will be served by honoring individual liberties.

So why is the same press, that is so protective of its chunk of the Bill of Rights, not willing to extend these same rights in their reporting to citizens on the other side of the First

Amendment? For example, why doesn't the press grant citizens Fifth Amendment rights during trial by press?

In my case, because of my misunderstanding of the mechanics of the press, and my misunderstanding of the capacity of the press to flat-out lie to the reader, I should have been granted the opportunity of counsel before being required to respond. I should have been given the press equivalent of Miranda rights.

This would be good journalistic practice for both the press and the accused. From a practical standpoint, let's take a well-known national example.

In January of 1995, Connie Chung of CBS interviewed Newt Gingrich's (the new Speaker of the House of Representatives) mother. At a point in the interview, Ms. Chung asked Ms. Gingrich what her son thought of the President's wife, Hillary Clinton. At first, Ms. Gingrich declined. But Ms. Chung pressed with the statement

> "why don't you just whisper it to me, just
> between you and me?"

Ms. Gingrich did.

Mistake.

Ms. Gingrich failed to read the rules.

Because it would turn out not to be just between Ms. Chung and Ms. Gingrich. Instead, CBS chose to televise this portion of the interview to a national viewing audience. And this huge audience heard, what Ms. Gingrich thought would be "just between you and me," that the Majority

Speaker of the United States House of Representatives thought the President's wife was a,

"bitch."

I am not kidding.

Unbelievable.

What happened to this country?

But, ridiculousness had not ended. After most folks expressed their outrage with such journalistic conduct, Eric Ober, the President of CBS was quoted as saying,

"While broadcasting Mrs. Gingrich's comments may have been perceived by some as unfair, CBS News does not believe withholding those comments would have been appropriate."

Not appropriate?

In other words,

"While as broadcasting Mrs. Gingrich's comments is ethically wrong to most folks, CBS News is trying to improve it's ratings."

This is yet another example of how the press is so out-of-touch with regular folks. It appears the press assumes regular folks somehow know the rules of the game. They assume that when a reporter makes a promise, we are to inherently know that such promises are invalid if it makes good copy. They seemed to be shocked to discover that such rules, so well-known and accepted among politicians, public personalities, and corporate leaders, might not be so well known to the general public.

They seemed to be shocked to discover that to many of us, a promise is a promise.

"Not appropriate?"

Therefore, to protect the press from criticism, and to protect citizens from self incrimination, I have a suggestion. I think any testimony by a citizen in trial by the press should be prefaced by Fifth Amendment warnings similar to that required in trial by law. For example, before Ms. Chung did the interview, Ms. Gingrich should have been informed,

- (1) You have the right to remain silent.
- (2) Anything you say can be used against you in the press, regardless of what Ms. Chung promises.
- (3) You have the right to a public relations firm and/or law firm, and to have this team present while you are being questioned.
- (4) If you cannot afford such a team, one will be provided to you, hopefully to be paid for after your son completes his book deal.

Then, if Ms. Gingrich still chose to have confidence that Connie Chung really meant to keep her word, Ms. Gingrich could then reasonably be faulted as being naive.*

The point is, trial by the press often has worse ramifications than trial by jury. Therefore, it seems to me that the press should make every effort to honor the rights of the accused, regardless if they are mothers of dastardly conservatives, or if they are members of the medical profession.

* (In fairness, it should be pointed out on April 7, 1995, Connie Chung/CBS was the only non-cable, national network to cover Newt Gingrich's speech, and the Democratic response after the historic first 100 days of the 104th Congress describing the Contract with America. ABC ran "Sister, Sister." And NBC ran "Unsolved Mysteries." In my judgement, the only unsolved mystery at NBC was why attaching ignition devices to trucks in order to fabricate a perspective was news, but the end of one of the most famous 100 days in congressional history was not news).

(4) DISCRIMINATORY PUBLIC CONDEM-NATION OF CITIZENS WITH SELECTED OCCUPATIONS IS WARRANTED IF THE AVERAGE INCOME OF THOSE OCCUPA-TIONS EXCEED THAT OF THE REPOR-TER.

Class warfare is wrong. Many of us who became successful did not start out that way. But either way, it shouldn't matter. No one who is monetarily successful should be subject to public ridicule based solely on income. And I must admit being increasingly intolerant of newspaper reporters, editors, and politicians who make more money than I, and who have better pension plans than I, espouse how I as a doctor, am:

- Overcharging patients.
- Not paying my fair share of taxes.
- Taking money from working families.

There comes a time when the truth needs to be told.

The bottom line is that if I had decided to become a reporter instead of a doctor, my abilities are such that I could have breezed through journalism classes in college, while achieving top-notched grades. And I could have done so with far less effort than required in premedical courses.

I could have had a lot more fun, and sacrificed a whole lot less.

Afterward, it is likely I would have been offered a low to moderate paying entry level job in journalism. And although the pay may not have been as high as a 40 year old doctor, it would have been enough to start a family somewhere between ages 22 - 25 years of age. Through the years, I would slowly move up the journalism ladder and be rewarded with a stable income, minimal loans, a pension plan, weeknights and weekends off, and with a growing family.

And if I worked hard, maybe I could become an editor making greater than $60,000 a year, or a Gannett corporate official making millions plus perks.

Contrast this life to that of being a doctor. I have worked since I was 14 years old. In high school, when I wasn't working, I spent many of my evenings and weekends studying while my friends were out having fun. I made the sacrifice.

In college, when I wasn't working, I spent many of my evenings and weekends studying while my friends were having fun. I made the sacrifice.

In medical school, four years of my life were dedicated to little else but becoming a doctor. And I would challenge anyone to find any profession that demands more academic requirements, more technical training, more loss of sleep, more emotional stress, more responsibility, and more commitment than that of becoming a doctor. And even though medical school was a sacrifice I willingly made, make no mistake, I made the sacrifice.

And even after four years of difficult high school courses, four years of difficult college courses, and four years of medical school, my medical training was not completed. I went on to three more years in Internal Medicine training, and another two more years in Endocrinology and Metabolism training. And despite 17 years of training since starting my science courses in high school, and despite working almost full time during my pre-medical school years, my entry into the real work place of private practice was first rewarded by a letter from the Administration Affairs office indicating I owed tens of thousands of dollars in student loans.

My second reward was answering, and being tied to a pager all night, and every week night, and every other weekend.

Finally, after several years of private practice I finally reached the financial stability where I could reasonably get married. At age 36, when my high school buddies' kids were getting ready to go to college, my wife and I were able to start having children.

But the sacrifice still didn't stop. During our first pregnancy, my wife was recommended to have blood testing performed for fetal surveillance. It was discovered that she had a low blood level of alpha fetoprotein. Her obstetrician indicated that this meant an increased risk of Downs syndrome, and she recommended an amniocentesis.

She stated to my wife that the risks were only one in two hundred. But even though I am a doctor, and even though my wife is an educated, professional woman, all either of us heard was the one, not the two hundred. We were devastated. We were convinced that our first child would be a Downs child. I desperately tried to find other risk factors that might influence our risk, pending the results of the amniocentesis (which was to take weeks).

> Downs syndrome n.., Mongolism, a variety of congenital, moderate to severe mental retardation. Marked by sloping forehead; presence of epicanthal folds causing an Oriental appearance of eyes; bridge of nose flat or sometimes absent; low-set ears; and generally dwarfed physique.

The major risk factor for the conception of a Downs child was age.

RISKS OF HAVING A DOWNS CHILD

MOTHER'S AGE	RISK OF DOWNS CHILD
20	1/1,667
25	1/1,250
30	1/ 952
35	1/ 378
40	1/ 106

Had I elected to be a journalist, and had the option of starting a family at age 27 years of age, my wife (who is seven years younger) would have been 20 years old and would have had a risk of a Downs child of $1/1,667$. But due to her age, and due to the low level of alpha fetoprotein, she and I were both convinced we were having a Downs child.

I knew that I had sacrificed much of my life towards becoming a doctor. This was my choice. But I had not realized that my sacrifice could lessen the chances that my wife and I would have a healthy child. And my question to reporters and editors who have such a pathologic and bizarre obsession of class warfare, how much money are their children worth?

Because I have sacrificed much of my life for the pursuit of curing the ill, I will not have the opportunity to share as many years with my children as those in journalism. So to all those at the Gannett Courier-Journal who were able to start their families in their twenties or earlier, and who have had years of enjoyment with their healthy children, how much money are those years worth?

And how much money is the increased chances of having *healthy children* worth?

I would challenge those at Gannett to attend my next medical school class picnic. While as other picnic gatherings elicits conversation of sporting events and gossip, my medical school classmates and spouses often focus their conversation on their problems with fertility. I do not know why so many women doctors, and so many spouses of men doctors have problems with fertility, but it sure seems disproportionately high. I suspect it goes back to the fact that so many in professional occupations choose to delay starting families due to the sacrifice required.

So my last question is, how much money is having the ability to have *children at all* worth?

I am just tired of it. The emotional trauma of the three weeks in which my wife and I waited for the amniocentesis results were even worse than the wrongful harm to my reputation and family from the irresponsible Gannett reporter. If the amniocentesis had proven positive for Downs, we had planned to have the child, care for the child, and love the child. But everyone dreams of having a healthy baby. And when I think of the utter callousness of reporters and editors who deliberately misstate the fact in an effort to harm my reputation and family - all because of their petty, pathologic and bizarre obsession with how much money I may, or may not make,

I am at a loss for words.

It seems to me, if the press wanted to find real instances where the desire for fortune and fame may be corruptive, they needn't look far. When the editors of newspapers choose the manner in which a headline is slapped across the front page, and choose the manner in which the story is written solely on the basis to sell newspapers, I think reasonable folks could see this as a potentially corrupt system.

To counter this obvious potential conflict of interest, one would think that the editors would be extremely cautious that stories against citizens were accurate to the last letter, and were fair as much as humanly possible - particularly if it was to be the front page, lead headline story of the day in the only state-wide newspaper. And if inaccuracies or unfairness did by chance occur, it would seem that the editors would make it policy to take extraordinary steps to correct the injustice, and to ensure that such reporting did not happen in the future.

It would seem that editors would have an uncompromising dedication to truth, and an unyielding respect and compassion for the reputation of the very citizens they had a constitutional obligation to protect - because it is the dedication to protecting individual liberties through reporting the truth that defines journalism as a profession.

And it is the demonstration of such dedication that gives journalism its credibility.

But obviously, my viewpoint is not necessarily shared by all in the press. Instead, many journalists find that destructive and cynical stories are major stepping stones to garnering more front page exposure to reach the ultimate goal of someday becoming a celebrity journalist.

On a local level, public television routinely features programs in which guest journalists from newspapers around the state sit around the table and agree with each other. They become celebrities. Opposing viewpoints to their "perspective" are not generally permitted. Balanced opinions are not the goal. And at the end of each program, they each leave the studio with the pious knowledge that they are far more ethical, far more insightful, and far more wiser than the rest of us poor slobs. After all, in their judgment, the only accurate and objective way to form a journalistic perspective is by forming those perspectives in discussions with other journalists.

And all the while, this shameless self promotion is little more than a chance to stroke each other's ego, and a chance to sell more newspapers.

On a national level, the lure of altering one's opinion in order to cash in on television dollars, and subsequent speeches, is even more tempting. To their credit, at least some of the talk shows do allow, and some insist on opposing opinions. I much prefer this situation to the "follow the leader," lemming mentality of the journalists on the local public television.

> Lemming: n., any of various small Arctic rodents resembling mice but having short tails and fur-covered feet: some species undertake spectacular mass migrations at peaks of population growth, ultimately following each other over cliffs into the sea to destruction.

But when some of the more lucrative television news shows desire journalists with extreme political positions, this introduces another clear potential conflict of interest. Does the lure of fame and fortune effect the opinion of journalists? According to Stephen Budiasky, Ken Bode, political director for ABC news has said,

> "Journalists are tempted to outbid each other
> in the opinions they express."

And the rewards for such extreme opinionated journalists are substantial. Regular journalists of "meet the Press," "The McLaughlin Group," and "Washington Week" are said to command a few thousand dollars to as high as $20,000 or more per speech on the lecture circuit.

So I feel compelled to ask the obvious. I would welcome anyone, particularly at Gannett, to explain to me why the income of doctors is worthy of front page public condemnation, when it is far less than many TV journalists, newspaper owners, or Gannett executives?

As a doctor, I can point to specific examples of actual human lives that I have saved. I can point to specific examples of horrible, human diseases that I have cured. I can point to specific examples of human suffering that I have relieved. I can point to specific examples of research that I have conducted that have benefitted patients. And my specific examples of making actual differences in actual human lives does not occur just once a week, but rather multiple times, every day.

So I ask, why is the level of doctor's monetary reimbursement an outrage that justifies deceitful and inaccurate front page condemnation, while as the high income of newspaper owners, editors, and newspaper corporate executives a proper and just payment for services rendered?

Reasonable folks might ask,

"Who is of greater worth to society?"

CHART OF CLASS WARFARE

Citizens worthy of front page condemnation based solely on income	Citizens not worthy of front page condemnation based solely on income
Doctors	Lottery winners
Female Prosecuting Attorneys	Female models
Small Business Owners	Artists
College Coaches	College Players Who Go Professional
Doctors	College Professors
Conservative Entertainers (i.e. Rush Limbaugh)	Liberal Entertainers (i.e. Barbara Streisand)
"For Profit" Hospital Administrators	"Not For Profit" Hospital Administrators
Government Officials	Newspaper Editors/ Owners
Corporate Executives	Corporate Gannett Executives
Doctors	Television News Celebrities
Doctors	Stand-up Comics
Doctors	Musicians
Doctors	Janitors
Doctors	Authors*

* Includes Democratic Vice Presidents, but not Republican Majority Leaders of Congress

(5) "GOTCHA" IS THE MOST ORGASMIC WORD IN JOURNALISM.

A journalistic climax occurs when, after months of foreplay in gathering evidence and statements from accusers, the reporter is finally able to make that call to the accused and savagely demand a heart-pounding and breathless response.

This orgasmic experience is known as "gotcha."

Medically speaking, the pursuit of orgasm is a primordial urge that drives the need of animals to procreate. In human beings, the pursuit of orgasm may also be solely for sexual pleasure.

Voluntary sex in humans is a primordial encounter that provides pleasure and gratification to both parties. Forced sex is considered a violent act that provides satisfaction to the aggressor, but horrible, lasting pain to the victim. Nevertheless, in animals, forced sex is not unusual. "Mounting" is often an example of forced sex that occurs in nature and that may be interpreted as an act of conquering, or act of demonstrating superior strength.

> Mount vt., to climb on (a female) for copulation: often said of an aggressive sexual act by a male animal

212

Business and government are not allowed to act solely on the basis of primordial urges. Reasonable restraints exist in our judicial system to harness these acts. However, the press has been given constitutional protection to act on their primordial urges, often without reasonable restraints. And while most journalists appreciate, respect, and do not abuse this privilege, other reporters conduct themselves in what can only be referred to as journalistic mounting.

"Gotcha" is an example of journalistic mounting.

Ah, but many reporters are young. And who can blame them if on a sunny spring day, their eyes and word-processors turn towards satisfying their primordial urges. But editors and newspaper owners are often older. And in their older years, they simply don't have the same primordial drive as their younger colleagues.

But that is not to say that editors and newspaper owners are not without passion. Rather, these passions have simply evolved. Specifically, while as a "gotcha" phone call imparts pleasure to the reporter, it is the manner in which "gotcha" articles are written and the manner in which they are presented that imparts pleasure to the editors and newspaper owners.

So while as reporters yearn for the sensual pleasures of "gotcha," editors and newspaper owners have their own desire. They want to see stories and headlines written and presented with:

"Edge."

"Edge" is another term used in journalism to denote a story or headline designed to shock, or make the reader take notice. And to achieve "edge," one of two things has to happen. If the subject of the story is truly guilty of a horrible crime, then simply reporting the gruesome details is often enough. But if the subject happens to be some innocent poor bastard who fell in the path of a "gotcha" starved reporter, then the "edge" is often created.

And in the language of most folks, this simply means taking a cheap shot. And these cheap shots fulfill two important needs of today's newspapers.

MARKETING

Strictly from a marketing standpoint, stories with "edge" and shock headlines sell newspapers. This is how corporate Gannett makes its millions/billions. Therefore, the choice of headline, and the choice of lead story is largely based on it's "sex appeal." It is therefore not unreasonable to assume that the need to sell newspapers influences decisions with regard to the content, and to the way the headline is presented - particularly the front page headline.

And it is not unreasonable to predict that the more the readerships of newspapers decline, the more marketing will influence how stories are written, and how they are presented. In the past years, the readership of the 10 largest newspapers (including some Gannett papers) has declined. This is an ominous prospect for those of us who have long been on Gannett's mounting list.

214

FOND MEMORIES

On the other hand, strictly from a journalistic standpoint, shock headlines also bring back memories of the Watergate break-in, which forever set the standard for investigative reporting. In this monumental event, the press demonstrated the absoluteness of their power by toppling the most powerful man on the planet - the President of the United States of America. But in trying to relive this most romantic period in journalism, it seems many editors have forgotten that the Watergate investigative reporters were extraordinary journalists who went through extraordinary efforts to seek documentation and confirmation of the facts before reporting the story. So while everyone remembers the reporting of the Watergate break-in as a monumental task, what seems to have been lost to many journalistic pretenders is that the tireless and relentless pursuit of truth was also a monumental task.

Woodward and Bernstein did not deserve their accolades because they simply fell into a story. Rather they deserve their accolades because of their work ethic and dedication to finding and reporting the truth despite the potential consequences.

And it is this dedication to protecting individual liberties through reporting the truth that defines journalism as a profession.

(6) AGENDA-MINDED EDITORIALIZING AND OPINION ARE OFTEN GIVEN PRIORITY OVER FACTS WHEN REPORTING THE NEWS

In the 1960 - 1980's, if you were to ask what's wrong with America, many folks would express the fears of heated ongoing wars, cold impending wars, and the risk of global nuclear destruction. It is not hard to remember all the movies, and all the Twilight Zone episodes examining the aftermath of the end of the world as a result of thermonuclear annihilation. But as these concerns have somewhat abated, we have begun to internalize our worries to focus on the inner problems in our society.

If you ask what's wrong with America in the 1990's, most folks believe that we have too much cynicism and whining, and too little accountability and responsibility. We have too many people bent on destruction, and not enough are concerned with construction. And since destructive behavioral problems are the main threat to our democratic system today, how much does the press contribute to the solution, and how much does the press contribute to the problem?

Today, I think most folks agree that the press spends far

too little time reporting inspirational stories of success, and far too much time reporting cynical stories of real or fabricated problems and failures. And it is this destructive behavior of the press that often gets in the way of society solving it's problems.

It should be made clear that such destructive conduct is not unique to the press. For example, politicians regularly ignore and/or ridicule the inspirational success stories of their rival political colleagues, as well as their constituents. Instead, too many politicians cynically accuse others of real or fabricated problems purely for political gain. And after the relentless and vicious attacks on the character of the voters who may have differing political viewpoints, I am amazed that these same politicians wonder why they don't get the admiration and respect from the public they feel they so richly deserve.

For example, I do not consider myself a right-wing conservative. I am a registered Democrat. And I believe that it is *personal conduct* that diminishes racism and that enhances volunteerism rather than rhetoric and good intentions.

In 1980, I voted for John Anderson instead of Ronald Reagan for President because I did not believe that our country could increase defense spending and cut taxes at the same time.

It seemed to me that this had the potential to create a budget deficit.

And after the election of Bill Clinton for President, I

believed he had done many positive things. I gave him credit for reducing the deficit in his first two years. I gave him credit for trying to downsize government to make it more efficient. I gave him credit for being an intelligent man, and a great campaigner.

But, whether intended or not, Bill (and Hillary) Clinton had personally worsened my life, and worsened the lives of other citizens as well.

When Ronald Reagan was President, he may have partially been responsible for exceeding the limit on the country's credit card, but at least he made us feel good while we were bankrupting the country. He inspired and honored those who sacrificed to become successful. If you worked hard and became successful, your family was proud of you, and you knew your President was proud of you. Ronald Reagan was a father-figure and king who re-affirmed that the American Dream was a great thing.

But under the Clintons, anyone who became successful, regardless of their personal sacrifices, were "not paying their fair share." If you were a hospital administrator, a health insurance worker, or a pharmaceutical worker, then you were a greedy bastard. If you were a small business owner, if you believed in the free enterprise system, or if you believed in a balanced budget, then you were a bigot who wanted to ignore the sick, and starve the children. If you believed in conservative social values, considered yourself a religious person, believed in limited government or if you believed in the 2nd Amendment of the Constitution, then you were a fanatic. If you believed that life begins at conception, if you believed you paid enough taxes or if you believed that people who work and give to society have earned a greater quality of life than those who don't work and take from society, then you are uncaring and intolerant.

In fact, the only people the Clintons apparently felt were worthy of their successes were attorney abortionists who were on some sort of government assistance program, and who liked McDonald cheeseburgers and fries, but who didn't represent anyone named Paula or Jennifer.

The point is, when Bill and Hillary Clinton were elected President, they were elected as representatives of all the people. The campaign was suppose to be over. The attacks on citizens were suppose to stop. But instead, the campaign did not stop and the most powerful couple in the world were aggressively making villains out of innocent citizens.

Why did it have to be this way? And when President Clinton and his political party (my President and my political party) have conducted themselves in this manner, how could they possibly blame others for being divisive.

Were they really that out of touch?

This was tragic on many levels. First of all, this irresponsible liberalism was destructive to the goals of responsible liberals. If President Clinton had spent more time condemning blatant acts of discrimination (such as many country club, racial exclusionary rules), and defending affirmative action programs granting consideration to the economically disadvantaged (which statistically would have disproportionately benefitted minorities), many of us who believe in civil rights could have been supportive. If he had agreed with a balanced budget from the beginning, but felt that reductions in the projected spending on education should be matched by reductions in the projected spending on defense (through improving efficiency - not services), I suspect most all Americans would have been supportive.

But when the President and his party (i.e. my president, and my party) repeatedly asserted that those of us who believed in a balanced budget were uncaring bigots (because we believed that current sacrifices were morally just to improve the future of our children), why is it so hard to understand that other accusations of potential true acts of bigotry no longer had an impact.

How had they forgotten the childhood lesson of "crying wolf."

But perhaps worst of all, their divisive rhetoric had enormous impact on the press. For example, it was during the Clintons' attack on the medical care providers that prompted the Gannett newspaper to wrongfully damage my family and reputation.

The point is, I wonder if Bill or Hillary Clinton had a clue that whenever they trashed a segment of Americans, the lemming mentality of the press is such that subsequent "human interest" stories using "real victims" would be blasted across the front pages of newspapers all over America, demonstrating how previously respected, successful, innocent citizens were really villains who deserved public humiliation and condemnation.

So as the direct result of the Clinton presidency, I have narrowed my requests of any future President to just three simple issues.

- Provide national and domestic protection.
- Be fiscally responsible.
- Leave me, and my family alone.

All I am asking of my government is that when I retire, I get at least some of the Social Security and Medicare benefits for which I have substantially invested in since age 14. And all I ask of my President is that he/she they quit prompting attacks by the press on my profession, my reputation, and thus my family.

It is unfortunate, but it is fact that unless government leaders back off the rhetoric, journalists will continue to rail on innocent citizens; because the press has little compassion for citizens on the other side of the First Amendment, and have little understanding of the impact their reporting has on peoples lives. In their hearts, they may think they are doing the right thing. But their work environment and culture is devoid of the reality of regular folk. It is therefore not an unexpected consequence that those in the press gradually lose touch.

The fact is, the First Amendment has created a wall that clearly divides those in the press from the rest of us folks. Specific members of the press do not fear legal liability, because they have constitutional protection that often eliminates reasonable challenges to their harmful acts. And they do not have to fear the press itself, because their colleagues feel that documented, specific wrongful acts of the press *are not* reportable, while as unproven, baseless, accusations of wrongful acts of business, government and citizens *are* reportable.

So while as accountability and responsibility represent reality to regular folks, because of the wall of the First Amendment, they represent just words on a page to those in the press.

I think that if the press was required to spend some time on this side of the First Amendment, I think they would be far more responsive towards providing truth, rather than promoting their thinly veiled bias and opinions in the non-editorial section of the newspaper.

(7) ALTHOUGH THE CONSTITUTION GRANTS THE PRESS THE OBLIGATION TO USE NEWSPAPERS AS A PROTEC- TOR OF INDIVIDUAL LIBERTIES, IT ALSO GRANTS THE PRESS A LEGAL LOOP- HOLE TO USE NEWSPAPERS AS A WEAPON AGAINST INDIVIDUAL LIBER- TIES.

Why don't libel laws protect citizens against wrongful acts of newspapers? The answer to this question is one of the most eye-opening aspects of my entire ordeal. The First Amendment of the Constitution states that,

> "Congress shall make no law...abridging the
> freedom of speech, or of the press..."

Our founding fathers believed that freedom of the press was necessary to democracy because it ensured citizens received truthful information. The intent was to grant the press freedom from governmental control and governmental influences. But if the press chose to abuse this privilege, citizens were granted the right recover damages through a suit of libel.

This seemed only fair.

As years have passed, the Supreme Courts have given great latitude to the press, even when wrongful and inaccurate information was reported. This latitude has been justified because it is presumed that a democratic society benefits from a press which has enormous "freedom" to report information that serves the public good.

As a result of this latitude, libel laws are slanted in favor of the press when public figures are involved. An example of such a decision can be found in New York Times v. Sullivan (1964). In an ad placed by a civil rights special interest group, the New York Times had published accusations that the police in Montgomery, Alabama had conducted a "wave of terror" against blacks. Because the ad contained specific errors regarding the details of the accusation, the city commissioner won a libel suit against the newspaper through a local Alabama jury in the amount of $500,000 in damages.

A jury of regular folks felt this decision represented justice.

However, the Supreme Court overturned the judgement in an unanimous decision. Because this case involved public officials, it was their judgement that the careless reporting of errors alone were not enough to prove libel. They therefore established the standard of:

"Actual malice."

The standard of "actual malice" requires that libel can only be proved if the inaccuracies were "with knowledge that it was false or with reckless disregard of whether it was false or not." Although this may seem reasonable, what has been the practical result of this opinion?

In his book, Make No Law, Anthony Lewis - a columnist for the New York Times, examined the Sullivan case and, not surprisingly, championed the decision.

Although I concede that much merit exists in protecting the press against unwarranted law suits for inadvertent mistakes against public or government officials, I wonder if Mr. Lewis realizes the countless, untold number of citizens who have their "pursuit of happiness" diverted, and their individual liberties trampled by a press that has used the Sullivan case in a most contemptible manner. The "freedom of the press" was granted as a privilege. The "freedom of the press" was intended to denote an obligation to protect individual liberties, not as a legal loophole to assault individual liberties.

In my case, the Gannett reporter clearly knew the facts, but chose to deliberately misstate the facts, even "with the knowledge that it was false." It would therefore seem that my case had fulfilled the standard of "actual malice."

Furthermore, in Sullivan, the Supreme Court's judgement concerned a public official. However, I was not a public official. I was just a doctor.

As such, it would seem that I had a clear opportunity to pursue full legal recourse with recovery of loss of income, loss of reputation and punitive damages.

Surely I could have nailed these guys.

Wrong.

It doesn't work that way in the real world.

The reason that citizens don't have a prayer against the press is multifold. First of all, I know of few citizens that could match the financial strength of the multibillion dollar Corporate Gannett. Secondly, while as the Supreme Court's decision had the well-intentioned goal to preserve an important component of democracy (the press), their decision has had the unintended practical effect of squashing any reasonable challenge to abuses of the press.

This is another example of how the First Amendment creates a wall that divides the press from the rest of us.

In business, if it is proven that an action of a company results in intentional harm, or results in reckless disregard for harm to citizens, then plaintiffs may be entitled to monetary recovery of legal fees, hospital fees, and loss of income. Furthermore, plaintiffs may also receive punitive damages meant to punish the defendant company with the goal to discourage such acts in the future.

In medicine, if it is proven that an action of a doctor results in intentional harm, or results in reckless disregard for harm to patients (i.e. malpractice), then plaintiffs may be entitled to monetary recovery of legal fees, hospital fees, and loss of income. Furthermore, plaintiffs may also receive punitive damages meant to punish the defendant doctor with the goal to discourage such acts in the future.

But in the press, if it is proven that an act of malice by a reporter results in intentional harm, or results in reckless disregard for harm to citizens, then it really doesn't matter.

From a practical standpoint, the ability to attain justice for wrongful acts of those in the press is next to impossible. And the press not only knows it, but flaunts it. In his letter of October 31, 1994, the Gannett Corporate Attorney responded to my suggestion that I might seek legal counsel unless Gannett was willing to acknowledge and make some attempt at atonement for their wrongful, front page, lead headline public condemnation of my reputation and family. His response was,

> "As you indicate in some of your letters, the media has substantial constitutional protection which will make any such litigation extremely difficult for you."

Furthermore, I was informed that if I did choose to litigate, Gannett would use its freedom granted by the constitution to further discredit my reputation and family by reporting those parts of the story which I,

> "apparently found distasteful."

After this letter, I did obtain legal counsel. Sadly, my attorney agreed with his assessment.

Hence, this confirmed that which I thought impossible in America.

Although the constitution grants the press the obligation to use newspapers as a protector of individual liberties, it also grants the press a legal loophole to use newspapers as a weapon against individual liberties.

(8) APOLOGY AND ATONEMENT FOR WRONGDOING IS ETHICALLY REQUIRED ONLY OF THOSE ON THE OTHER SIDE OF THE FIRST AMENDMENT.

The Bill of Rights was meant to create equality among citizens. But as stated before, the decisions of the Supreme Court that have granted great latitude to the press have also created a great wall dividing this nation into two separate groups - the press and regular folks.

Those in the press have constitutional protections that are granted to no one else.

Having been given this great gift, one would think the press would be grateful for this honor, and cognizant of the obligations of such a privilege. And if wrongful acts of the press were found to occur, even in the slightest of degrees, most folks would expect the press would go nuts in their apologies for any hint of such injustice.

But obviously, this doesn't always happen.

Instead, the precious gift of "freedom of the press" is used less and less to promote democracy, and more and more to foster arrogance among those in the press. Editors and newspaper owners anoint themselves as the sovereign judge in the decisions of which wrongful and inaccurate stories against citizens warrant due consideration, and which are simply cast aside.

But the "freedom of the press" was granted for the intent to protect individual liberties of *citizens*, not to feed the egos of reporters and editors. And as such, it seems reasonable to me that any misstatements in stories of wrongdoing by an accused citizen should be publicly corrected if, *in the viewpoint of the citizen,* the inaccuracy resulted in personal harm to income, reputation, and/or family. The decision should not be left up to the same reporter, editor, or newspaper owner who wrote or approved the injustice in the first place.

Furthermore, the correction should be published in at least the same prominence as the original story.

This would be fair.

And this would in no way diminish the ability of the press to fulfill its constitutional obligation to inform and promote the public good. Rather, because it would enhance the fulfillment of this goal by insuring that the truth would be told, and that individual liberties were protected. And, as a positive spin-off, it might encourage reporters to develop a greater dedication in reporting the facts. Because the press would be more accountable, they might become more responsible.

And who knows, it might even bring those in the press a little closer to this side of the First Amendment.

Just think about the ramifications. Imagine if the public had confidence that the press adhered to a simple policy of insuring truth in reporting. Just imagine if the public felt the press truly believed that it is the dedication to protecting individual liberties through reporting the truth that defines journalism as a profession. I think this would enhance the press' ability to meet its constitutional obligation - and democracy would be better served.

(9) EXPOSING THE WRONGDOINGS AND UNETHICAL BEHAVIOR OF THE CORPORATIONS AND GOVERNMENT OFFICIALS IS A CONSTITUTIONAL OBLIGATION; EXPOSING THE WRONG-DOINGS AND UNETHICAL BEHAVIOR OF THE CORPORATE PRESS IS INAPPRO-PRIATE.

Envision you were a reporter. Suppose one day you were provided evidence that a powerful corporation had repeatedly and deliberately acted to harm citizens for the sake of self-promotion, and economic gain. In addition, you had clear evidence that included extensive documentation describing the deceit and corruption of the corporation, as well as letters from corporate attorneys threatening any innocent victim who dared challenge the wrongful acts of this multibillion dollar corporate machine.

And finally, you even had in your possession an admission of guilt from the Vice President of the corporation.

Given such a story, it is probable every investigative, journalistic, rabid drop of blood in your body would froth

232

with passion as you wrote the front page, lead headline story of the day:

> "CITIZENS WRONGFULLY HARMED BY GREEDY AND CALLOUSED COR- PORATION"

(For this imaginary scenario, we will leave the orgasmic "gotcha" aspect alone for now.)

And as you wrote the story, imagine your confidence as you knew that despite any corporate threats, you could bravely proceed with the story, standing proudly behind the impenetrable First Amendment.

Imagine how just this would be. Imagine how great this would feel.

But at this point, you might recall that this kind of reporting goes on all the time. This kind of reporting is nothing new. Everyday in America, some calloused corporation, or some corrupt government agency or official is being brought to justice in trial by the press. And it is the obligation to report such injustices that helps the press insure democracy. And it is this accountability that helps promote responsibility in our society.

So what's the point?

Well, now consider the same situation, except now consider if that the multibillion dollar corporation owned and ran nationwide newspapers. Would this effect your courageous- ness as a reporter? Is there a different standard for reporting specific instances of wrongdoings of the corporate press than compared to specific instances of wrongdoings of other corporations?

I think there is.

I think there is a big difference.

Think about it. How many government and corporate officials have been accused of specific acts of wrongdoing on the front page of your local newspaper in the past week? I suspect the answer would be,

"a lot."

But how many reporters, editors, and/or press corporations have been specifically accused of acts of wrongdoing on the front page of your local newspaper in the past week?

Past month?

Past year?

Past decade?

Past millennia?

I suspect the answer would be,

"not a lot."

In my case, the Gannett Courier-Journal had been documented to have deliberately harmed my reputation and family in a significantly fabricated, front page, lead story of the day. However, despite the great wall of the First Amendment, and despite the threats from the Corporate Gannett attorney, I was determined to clear my name. Because I thought injustice by the corporate press was every bit as newsworthy as injustice by corporations, I wrote many of the national news organizations.

I wrote 60 Minutes (CBS).

I wrote Dateline (NBC).

And I even wrote Sam Donaldson at Primetime (ABC).

It was my argument that much had been written, and much has been discussed as to the distinct line of credibility between the "traditional media" (newspapers, networks, etc.) and the "new media" (tabloids, talk radio, etc.) with regard to standards of reported accuracy, and journalistic professionalism.

It was my argument that most folks would consider Corporate Gannett as a member of the select "traditional media." And in this age of class warfare, I felt that my case was an illustrative example of how this former janitor's life has been harmed by a calculated, deliberate act of libel that occurred under the new regime of Gannett - solely because I have made the unfortunate career choice to be a doctor in Kentucky.

I sent documents and newspaper clippings of how the Gannett Courier-Journal wrongfully harmed my reputation, family, and medical practice in a front page, lead headline story. I explained that this story was an inaccurate "perspective" article that contained deliberate fabrications of the essential facts regarding my involvement.

I also sent documents and newspaper clippings describing how the very same reporter subsequently was again found guilty of another inaccurate, front page, lead headline story implying greed on the part of university doctors who work in clinics to help the poor. This included the reports of Gannett's own writing staff publicly criticizing their own reporter and editors in printed form.

I noted the lack of response of Gannett editors to my protests, the censorship of my "letter to the editor," as well as the threats of the Gannett Corporate attorney. Finally, I enclosed the letter of apology from Gannett that fulfilled their requirement to apologize in an out of court settlement to avoid an in court libel suit.

My reason for writing these respected news shows was because, although the facts clearly documented wrongdoing, no one at Gannett had yet publicly condemned the deliberate nature of this injustice, nor publicly atoned for the deliberate nature of this injustice. And in fact, the same dangerous reporter who had repeatedly and wrongfully harmed innocent citizens was, and continues to be rewarded with several subsequent front page publications.

And in the end, I stated,

> "Much has been written and much has been discussed as to the distinct line of credibility between the "traditional media" (newspapers, networks, etc.) and the "new media" (tabloids, talk radio, etc.) with regard to standards of reported accuracy, and journalistic professionalism."

> "If you were standing on this side of the First Amendment, where would you draw the

line?''

And what was the response?

I received no response.

Surprised?

And I wonder. What would the response have been if, instead of writing about abuses of the press, I had written about abuses of a drug company? As a doctor and researcher of metabolic treatments, what would have been the response of the media if I had sent numerous documents confirming that a multibillion dollar drug company had intentionally been making drugs that repeatedly harmed patients. And I wonder what the response would have been if I had even included a letter from the Vice President of the company, admitting that such injustices were taking place.

What would have been the response?

A return letter, or phone call perhaps?

Would anyone be surprised?

But because I was sending information concerning a specific wrongful act of Gannett, I received no response. These news organizations did not write back to say that my case was boring. They did not say it was uninteresting. They did not say it was unimportant. They didn't even say that I was wrong. But instead, I guess they felt that any reporting against corporate Gannett, even with documentation of an admission of guilt was inappropriate.

I have thought long and hard as to why the networks had

forsaken me, and had felt that reporting the injustice against me was inappropriate.

Perhaps they thought that while as corporate injustice is front page news, *corporate press* injustice is no news.

Perhaps they felt that *any* criticism of the press is inappropriate, regardless of the atrocity. (And you can bet that any press person reading this book is simply writing it off as "press bashing").

Or perhaps they were scared of Gannett. I can certainly sympathize. It is conceivable that Gannett holds so much power, that it would be financially foolish for a even television network to challenge this multimillion dollar giant. But it should be remembered that television news departments have no fear of governmental or corporate officials due to First Amendment rights. And it would be most ironic if the very freedoms that were intended to protect individual liberties, also served to protect the multibillion dollar corporate press as they dismantle individual liberties.

(10) JOURNALISM IS NO LONGER A PROFESSION.

I believe that I am not alone in my objections to the press. I have tried to illustrate my frustrations in a case study of my own personal experience. I have also tried to use other well known examples to broaden the scope.

As stated before, it is likely that most of those involved with the press will simply write this off as "press bashing." But I think that would be a mistake. Speaking as a citizen who has never held public office and who, before this episode, had no particular ax to grind, there seems to be a ground-swell of anger towards the mainstream media that is unprecedented.

For proof, one needs to look no further than the flock of listeners to talk radio. I think many folks intrinsically know that they are often not being provided the truth, or at least the whole truth by the traditional media. That is why I believe that the traditional press is fading. Folks are tired of being fed opinionated newsreporting rather than unbiased facts. Folks feel that the deliberate misstatement of fact to achieve a perspective is an arrogant act of elitism.

And by choosing "perspective" over accuracy, the press is

losing it's credibility. And the more their credibility is challenged, the more the press reacts by even greater distortions, further compromising their credibility.

Will it go round in circles?

And due to this loss of credibility, it is both fortunate, and unfortunate that many folks simply don't believe the press anymore.

Fortunately, as a member of the wrongfully accused, I am now very grateful people are skeptical, even to the point of being cynical with regard to trusting the press - at least with regard to the Gannett Courier-Journal. And from a personal standpoint, I can certainly say that I will never again read an investigative report from the Gannett Courier-Journal with any confidence that it represents the truth. As long as the current reporters and editors remain entrenched in their vigilante mentality, I will choose to ignore their "perspective" articles until the real truth emerges in the "letter to the editor" section.

That is, if Gannett chooses not to censor such letters.

But even though I am thankful that many folks ignored the article about me because of the dwindling confidence in the Gannett Courier-Journal, I do not think this cynicism best serves the public good.

However, I see changes on the horizon. The age of "the new media" is just beginning. Yes, much of the new media is junk (tabloids, etc.). However, other forms of the new media provide a level of service and information that is not provided in the traditional media. A perfect example is C-Span. C-Span is a cable program that airs entire conversations, entire speeches, and entire proceedings of government. When I first began watching C-Span, I was astounded at the difference of what I heard in listening to a 45 - 60 minute speech, compared to the 15 second edited version of the same speech on the network news, or the description of the speech in the newspaper the next morning.

It was as though the press and I had seen two entirely different speeches.

Suddenly, Bill Clinton was no longer the sex-starved, indecisive boob who lacked direction and conviction. Suddenly, Newt Gingrich was no longer a right-winged bigot who only wanted to starve small children. And the most enlightening, and the most frightening aspect of all was,

> How accurate were my opinions about political leaders before C-Span?

It has become clear to me that many in the press cover only those aspects of political events that achieve their pre-conceived "perspective." Why does the press find it so hard to put their egos second, and the facts of the story first? It is this inability of the press to keep the facts in, and keep themselves out of the news that gives the appearance of "elitism."

Where is Walter Cronkite when you need him?

And the attack on this "elite" press is in no small way a contributing factor in the success of recent conservative politicians. The press seems oblivious to the fact that their biased and unfair attacks often work to their own disadvantage.

During the 1988 Presidential campaign, (then) Vice President George Bush agreed to a presidential "candidate profile," by Dan Rather of CBS news. But when the cameras began to roll, Mr. Rather sought to ambush Mr. Bush with questions solely directed at the Vice President's alleged involvement in Iran/Contra. Mr. Rather had little interest in conducting the "candidate profile" as originally promised, because he had the "perspective" that Vice President Bush was guilty of something. Therefore, any conduct that promoted his perspective was felt to be good, ethical journalism. Misleading the Vice President (the accused) about the nature of the story was felt to be good, ethical journalism. Harming the reputation of the Vice President through unsubstantiated allegations, and without supporting facts, was felt to be good, ethical journalism. ("Mr. Vice President, you've made us hypocrites in the face of the world. How could you sign on to such a policy?"). But Mr. Rather's relentless need to achieve his perspective over his obligation to report the truth was not interpretted as good, ethical journalism by the American public. Instead, Mr. Rather was perceived to be downright rude. Finally, in a classic moment in politics, Mr. Bush shot back with:

> "It's not fair to judge my whole career by a rehash on Iran. How would you like it if I judged your career by those seven minutes when you walked off the set in New York. How would you like that?"

By seizing the opportunity to expose the unfairness and hypocrisy of the "elite" press, George Bush buried his "wimp" image. And it should be remembered that George Bush was a war hero. But despite his acts of valor in combat, he was only able to shake the image of being a "wimp" when he engaged the press. It says much about public cynicism when standing up to the press says more about a person's courage than acts of mortal combat.

It also could be said that the landslide 1994 congressional elections were also partially attributable to Newt Gingrich's (Speaker of the House of Representatives), ability to tap into the public frustration with the "status quo," which was shamelessly championed by many in the national press. And, not unsurprisingly, because Mr. Gingrich had repeatedly challenged the "elite press," he had received unflattering editorials, hurtful caricatures, and flat-out misstatements. But what the press failed to understand was that the more Mr. Gingrich was wrongfully condemned for the sake of promoting an agenda or "perspective," the less the press was believed concerning other issues (Deceive me once, shame on you. Deceive me twice, shame on me).

Listen to radio talk-show conservative Rush Limbaugh on any given day. Listen to how many times he assumes the role as the leader in the fight of "us versus them." His followers believe him to be one of the few brave soles who is entrenched against the onslaught of distortions by the "main-stream media." And what his opponents fail to understand is that his claims of hypocrisy are based on specific examples of documented *truth*. This is what brings him credibility. Make no mistake, Rush Limbaugh is beyond all else an entertainer. But his credibility as a political analyst is based on his use of facts, and exact quotes of those he lampoons, rather than fabrications of facts to create a perspective. So although many may disagree with his analysis of the facts, or his interpretation of quotes, the reason so many well-informed Americans listen to Mr. Limbaugh is because he backs up many of his points with documented facts. And it is the dedication to reporting the truth that defines journalism, and that gives journalism its credibility.

Truth.

Hey Gannett.

Truth is where it's at in the 90's.

And it is the dedication to protecting individual liberties through reporting the truth that defines journalism as a profession.

This was the way it was supposed to be.

The point is, if distortions, and the expression of political opinions are the goal, then such opinions should be reserved for shows such as "Crossfire," "McLaughlin Group," and "Capital Gang" where attacking and defending through yelling and hollering is fun sport. But when the goal is to seek out the news, those in the press should take a second look at the Sunday morning news shows. "Face the Nation" and "David Brinkley" are examples of news shows that serve to bring government and issues to the people. These kind of news shows fulfill the constitutional obligations as originally intended by our Founding Fathers.

These news shows seek the truth.

And special mention should be made of "Meet the Press" with Tim Russert. I know of no news program that spends more time emphasizing the news guest/s over the egos of the reporters. Before he was moderator, Tim Russert was among one of the most dominant and sometimes ruthless reporters on television. But now that he is moderator, he repeatedly places the news far in front of his ego. This is a much under-recognized accomplishment. Quite frankly, the name "Meet the Press" has become somewhat of a misnomer. Because of Tim Russert, the show should be entitled "Meet the Newsmakers." As such, this is another example of excellence in journalism that should not go without notice.

And the presence of such excellence is in direct contrast to the "elites" who feel that their "perspectives" matter more than truth.

And this isn't just my opinion.

In 1994, James P. Gannon retired as Chief of the Detroit News' Washington Bureau. Included in his July 24, 1994 article ''A Fight for the Soul of Newspapers, Sensationalism and Gimmicks are Overtaking Responsibility,'' Mr. Gannon stated:

> ''At the end of this month, I will leave daily journalism after 33 years as a reporter, columnist, bureau chief and editor, to begin

work on a book.

The news business has been good to me and I leave it with gratitude, a sense of accomplishment and no regrets. I am not going away mad. But I am going away concerned about trends in the news business that I believe are harmful to the health of quality journalism.

There are powerful forces reshaping the news media in this country. In an age when newspaper readership is declining and the audiences for network news programs are falling, owners and managers of media properties are rightfully concerned about their future. In a desperate search for audience, they are increasingly substituting entertainment values for news values.

As a result, we are substituting sensation for significance and style for substance. Too often, we are combining the attributes of the tabloid newspaper and the TV talk show into a lowest-common-denominator form of journalism that cheapens our products and trivializes our professional purpose...,

I am not saying all is lost for journalism. There is plenty of outstanding newspapering being done. So we have not lost our souls. but there is a struggle under way for the future of journalism - and many respected veterans of our business believe the struggle is being lost. I believe that what has happened to television, where the battle is all but lost, is spilling over into newspapers, where it is under way...,

Newspaper editors are taking too many cues

from television. Just because a topic is a ratings success on Oprah or Donahue doesn't mean it belongs on Page One of a serious newspaper. Newspapers make a mistake trying to compete with television for sensation and titillation. TV can do that better than we can. We can do serious reporting on complex subjects better than TV can. We can provide readers more detail, more useful information, more insight, and more value for their nickel than TV can. We can't out-trash TV, and we shouldn't try.

I think we seriously underestimate our readers. I believe they are more interested in hard news and helpful information than many editors think they are. I think they care more about everyday problems of ordinary people than about the bizarre problems of celebrities. And I think they look to newspapers for this kind of helpful, serious news that they don't get on television - and are disappointed when they find a second-day version of TV titillation in their newspapers..."

This article appeared in the Gannett Courier-Journal just weeks after the significantly fabricated, front page, lead headline story that harmed my reputation and family. Afterwards, even though the readers had no way of knowing of the wrongful acts of Gannett against me, I was somewhat comforted by the readers' response to Mr. Gannon's article.

After his article was published, letters to the editor poured into the Gannett Courier-Journal. These published letters included:

"The print media have fallen into disrepute. As a newspaper junkie and a person who has read most of the big-city publications, I think I know some of the reasons.

First of all, newspapers are profit-making enterprises and therefore oriented toward whatever increases circulation and, consequently, allows higher advertising rates. To this end, stories with sensational subject matter tend to be favored by editors over those with more sober and better researched content. Thus infuses the publication with tabloid flavor that is offensive to serious readers.

Second, many newspapers have a definitely liberal tilt and tend to emphasize that aspect of the news over more conservative elements. Most consumers of print news hold a decidedly moderate or conservative point of view and are regularly disappointed, and disagree, with what they see in their newspapers.

Third, the integrity of many newspapers and reporters is questionable. Stories are poorly researched and have false or incomplete information presented as factual. News is slanted to serve the editorial agenda or political bias of the paper . . .

The mature and intelligent news consumer wants balanced, accurate and well-researched articles about important events and ideas that provide information to live by, not fluff to entertain, or titillate... Your charter is to provide true, accurate, balanced, and complete reporting on what is happening in the world. You are not suppose to influence us; you are suppose to inform us. We'll make good decisions if we have good information to work with..."

(A.L.H. Murray, Ky.)

"It will be a sad day for journalism when James Gannon retires. Journalism is fast becoming what the writer thinks the reader wants, not the actual facts. We are getting a warped, distorted view of our world as reality is being sacrificed for the sake of sensationalism...

If tabloid journalism is the wave of the future for newspapers, God help us. I'll support a constitutional amendment to limit freedom of the press and other media."

(K.J.B. Louisville Ky.)

"It was with great interest that I read James Gannon's July 24 article. In fact, I found myself actually nodding yes as I read more and more of the article.

It would appear that all the news media are competing for the top spot in sensationalism...

If the newspapers underestimate their audience, they can only hope to follow in the footsteps of the sleazy tabloids and TV shows, which are growing in number but surely must flame out and crash after a short and odious existence...

I hope newspapers continue to accept the challenge of responsible and factual, unbiased coverage of all stories they cover and print...

(R.W. Louisville Ky.)

James P. Gannon is right on target. His commentary made my day. His being a veteran journalist made it even better. He really told it the way things are.

Where are facts, truth and unbiased opinions these days? The news media (TV and newspapers) are a joke and an insult to one's intelligence...

(Mrs. H.M.F. Louisville)

It is strange to me that the media have so little trust in the integrity and good sense of the American people.

As any good journalism student, or up to a seasoned editor, knows - just report the facts. "Who, what, where, how and when" belong in the news section. "Why" is reserved for the editorial page!

> The media seem to have adopted that old
> nonsensical philosophy that "the end justifies
> the means." I have long since quit watching
> the news on television, and it looks like The
> Courier-Journal is on shaky ground...

(A.B.M. Louisville Ky.)

Virtually all letters expressed a similar frustration. I wonder how more frustrated they would have been if Gannett were required to disclose the untold number of "agenda over truth," or "perspective over accuracy" atrocities they had committed. Unfortunately, these unjust acts are forever secretly held in a sealed black box on their side of the First Amendment. Citizens, such as myself, have little reasonable way to let the truth be known.

Nevertheless, many folks clearly get the sense that something is not right. I agree. The First Amendment has not only created a wall between those in the press and the rest of us, but has also created a wall between what editors and reporters think they believe, and how they act.

For example, I think many in the press would agree with Mr. Gannon. However, they likely believe it is others in the press who are at fault - not them. For example, I have all confidence that those at the Gannett Courier-Journal are probably quite proud of their dedication to "ethics."

Afterall, didn't they publish Mr. Gannon's article? Didn't they publish the readers' response? Surely publishing ethical viewpoints absolves them from having to conduct their reporting in an ethical manner.

The point is, even though the press is often big on accepting criticism in a general sense, they are not so big on accepting criticism on specific acts. The First Amendment has not only established a wall between those in the press and the rest of us folks, but it also has apparently created a wall in the brain that divides the actual actions of editors from how they think they act.

It's just another brick in the wall.

For example, after my numerous letters and meetings with Gannett concerning the significantly fabricated, front page, lead headline story against me that wrongfully harmed my reputation and family, one would have expected that Gannett would have gotten the message.

Shortly afterward, Mr. Gannon's article was published. An outpouring of letters were received by the Gannett Courier-Journal venting the public's cry that the press consider truth and accuracy over perspective. One would have surely expected that Gannett would have gotten the message.

But they didn't get it.

Within weeks, the same Gannett Courier-Journal reporter, under the same editors who wrongfully harmed my reputation and family, again published another significantly misleading, front page, lead headline story. I wonder what must occur for Gannett to realize that it is the dedication to protecting individual liberties through reporting the truth that defines journalism as a profession?

CHAPTER 5:

IT CAN HAPPEN, BUT WHAT CAN BE DONE?

"I had meetings. I sent letters. I made phone calls. I did everything I could to try and achieve justice. But in the end, justice was thwarted, not because of my lack of will or lack of justification, but because of the First Amendment of the Constitution. But I do not believe that the First Amendment was meant to be a legal loophole for an irresponsible press."

RESPONSIBILITY AND ACCOUNTABILITY

Responsibility, even among the most ethical and noble, is best achieved through accountability. And in America, we believe that no one should be above being held accountable.

No one, and no institution.

Justice is blind.

That is a basis of justice.

Doctors have a responsibility to cure, and/or treat the sick. At the same time, doctors must be accountable. Those who deliberately commit harmful acts against patients may be subject to "malpractice" law suits, with punitive awards sometimes in millions of dollars. But beyond potential financial accountability, we in medicine have an ethical responsibility as well. That is why physicians such as myself volunteer to provide medical care to the homeless, and are actively involved in other charitable causes.

Muscians have a responsibility to perform. At the same time, musicians must be accountable. Those who deliberately blast the crowd with ear-hemorrhaging, inappropriate noise in an effort to ruin wedding receptions, holiday functions, or otherwise fail to keep their obligation may be

subject to non-payment. Furthermore, wrongful performances may negate future "gigs," with long-term loss of
income. But beyond potential financial accountability, we
in music have an ethical responsibility as well. That is why
so many in music volunteer their talents to help raise funds
for the hungry and AIDS.

Stand up comics have a responsibility to entertain. At the
same time, comics must be accountable. Those who
deliberately rail on the audience to ruin a comedy show fail
to fulfill their obligation to entertain and may be subject to
non-payment. Furthermore, childish conduct may negate
future "gigs," with long-term loss of income. But beyond
potential financial accountability, we in comedy have an
ethical responsibility as well. That is why so many in
comedy volunteer their talents to help raise funds for the
homeless.

Janitors have a responsibility to clean. At the same time,
janitors must be accountable. Those who deliberately leave
unswept carpets, greasy floors, and unsanitary bathrooms
fail to keep their obligation to clean, and may be subject to
non-payment. Furthermore, repeated inadequate performance may result in getting fired with long-term loss of
income. But beyond financial accountability, we who have
been janitors have an ethical responsibility as well. That is
why so many janitors, and other laborers, spend so much of
their time helping their neighbors and family.

But what about the press?

Those in the press have the constitutional responsibility to protect individual liberties by reporting the truth. But in contrast to virtually every other occupation imaginable, they often have no reasonable accountability. Furthermore, if they are the only state-wide newspaper, then they have a monopoly status that prevents concerns regarding loss of income.

And beyond the financial accountability, those in the press often have no reasonable requirement to publicly atone, nor even publicly acknowledge, wrongful acts. And if admission of wrongful acts are granted by the all-powerful press, such corrections are often half-hearted and buried in the "You'll-Never-See-It" section of the newspaper.

This is unfair, and unjust.

But it should not be surprising. Any institution that is granted unique and special privileges has the potential to abuse these privileges. The First Amendment grants the press the unique and special privilege of almost absolute power.

And if power corrupts, then absolute power corrupts absolutely.

So what can be done?

How can the press be held responsible and accountable, but yet assure that the "freedom of the press" is protected.

I have two suggestions.

To **Prof Butler**

Date _____ Time _____

IMPORTANT MESSAGE

M _Thought you_

of _might enjoy_

Phone _reading This —_

TELEPHONED		PLEASE CALL	
RETURNED CALL		WILL CALL AGAIN	
WANTS TO SEE YOU		URGENT	

Message _"Libel Laws" p257_
"10 Rules --- Irresp. Press
_p. 274_

JET SPEED
PRINTING CO.

1000 N. Lansing St.   PHONE (517) 224-6475
St. Johns, MI 48879-1054   FAX (517) 224-3148

BRING BACK LIBEL LAWS

Many would agree that inaccurate, or misleading statements reported without harmful intent should not be subject to huge monetary awards, particularly if the press corrects these inaccuracies promptly, fairly, and in good faith. This is especially true when such reporting concerns government or public officials.

However, if inaccurate or misleading statements by the press are reported with intended harm against a *citizen*, if these inaccuracies are not corrected promptly, fairly, and in good faith, and if such actions fulfill the standard of "actual malice," then current libel laws need to be weighted more in favor of citizens. As it stands now, unless a sizable loss of income can be conclusively proven, citizens who are libeled are often advised to drop the matter because the press has an unfair advantage with regard to a twisted constitutional interpretation of the "freedom of the press."

If the corporate press is guilty of harming the reputation of citizens due to intentional misstatements designed to "create a perspective," then citizens should have no less opportunity to be awarded loss of income, loss of reputation, and punitive damages as would surely occur with virtually any other corporation.

And I know many in the press feel that libel suits are already too frequent - and often frivolous - even with the constitutional protections. But as a doctor who practices in a field with no constitutional protection, and who practices in an environment in which frequent and frivolous lawsuits are not only more common, but sought out in advertisements, I admit having very little sympathy for the multi-billion dollar press industry.

In my experience, the number of libel suits against the press is far too few, particularly regarding injustice against citizens. And if the press was required to be more accountable, they would surely be far more responsible with the truth, or they would be litigated into closure. But, since the press is not reasonably accountable, they can afford to be reckless with the truth. And this, in no small way, accounts for the low emphasis of truth and fairness by many in the press.

So why can the press act in such an irresponsible manner?

Because they know they can.

Also, it should be noted that the financial situation of many in the press has dramatically changed, In the past, the press was less frequently owned and operated by big money corporate machines. Hence, allowing frequent, and large libel suit awards could have conceivably shut down many important providers of news. And because most agree that the press fulfills an important role in protecting individual rights in a democratic society, such awards were best avoided.

However, much of the press of today bears little resemblance to that of yesterday. Much of the press is now owned and operated by multi-billion dollar corporations. It is inconceivable to me why that individual citizens and small business are susceptible to career-ending and company-closing punitive damages for wrongful acts, while as the multi-billion dollar press machine is often exempt from similar awards in libel suits.

A viable business environment is vital for a growing democracy. But, in business, intentional wrongful acts against the individual rights of citizens may result in plaintiff recovery of legal fees, and loss of income, as well as possible punitive damages meant to punish the defendant company with the goal to discourage such acts in the future. And if the business closes as the result of such monetary awards, then so be it. Protection of individual liberties is guaranteed by our constitution. It is the basis of law.

A thriving medical environment is vital for a healthy public. But, in medicine, intentional wrongful acts against citizens may result in plaintiff recovery of legal fees, hospital fees, and loss of income, as well as possible punitive damages meant to punish the defendant with the goal to discourage such acts in the future. And if the doctor or hospital closes as the result of such monetary awards, then so be it. Protection of individual liberties is guaranteed by our constitution. It is the basis of law.

A free press is also vital for a growing and healthy democracy and public. But, in the press, intentional wrongful acts against citizens is often a non-prosecutable offense. For reasons unclear, it has become acceptable for businesses, doctors, and everyone else in society to be severely sanctioned for wrongful acts, but it has become unacceptable, or "inappropriate" for the press to be so sanctioned. The press is not required to honor individual liberties in their reporting. They have the freedom to largely ignore the basis of law.

Therefore, in view of the changing status of the press, and in view of the numerous other (ever-expanding) media sources available, I believe the time has come for Congress to consider legislation to introduce today's press into the real world. I think it is time for Congress to allow wrongfully accused citizens the same opportunity to recover damages against the corporate press as with any other corporation in America. The libel laws need to be re-written to pass the "salivation standard." In other words, when I approached my attorney with a clear case of libel that I felt met the Supreme Court standard of "actual malice," he should have been as excited (i.e. hungry to the point of salivation) as if I had approached him with a clear case of medical or corporate malpractice.

And in the sense that the First Amendment is a constitutional obligation, any act of "actual malice" should be a far more serious, and prosecutable offense than other lawsuits.

Therefore, I call on my elected representatives to help protect individual liberties by holding the press more accountable for their actions, as truly intended in the Constitution. This would not impair the "freedom of the press." The press would continue to be able to print anything they wanted, as long as it was the truth.

However, if the press, with actual malice, intentionally reported misstatements against citizens in order to achieve a perspective, or to simply create a headline to sell more newspapers, then the multi-billion dollar press industry should be held accountable - financially. Not only would this improve the chances of responsible journalism, but it would fulfill the true intent of the Bill of Rights.

And best of all, if the press were subject to a similar degree of accountability as the rest of us, I make a prediction. I predict that if the press was required to spend some time on this side of the First Amendment, the attitude of reporters and editors would undergo a dramatic philosophical change.

Currently, editors and reporters enjoy a dream world that is separated from reality by "the freedom of the press." If the press was required to be as accountable for their actions as the rest of us folks, I predict that within a very short period of time, the so-called "irresponsible liberal bias" would quickly fade. Because when there is no accountability, there is little incentive to be responsible. It is in this environment that irresponsible attitudes are allowed to flourish. However, once accountability, and thus responsibility was required, I think you would find that the press would again become a most honored, and respected institution.

And if they maintained a liberal bias, at the least, their bias would be based on a similar degree of responsibility as is expected from other folks on this side of the First Amendment. And their biases (be they liberal or be they conservative) would be closer to that of the citizens whose individual liberties they have an obligation to protect.

PASS THE "THE UNIFORM CORREC-TION OR CLARIFICATION OF DEFAMA-TION ACT" (See Appendix)

While as punitive monetary awards are perhaps the quickest, and the most effective ways to promote accountability, and induce responsibility, this often misses the point. For many of us who have been wronged by the press, all we want is for the press to report the truth.

However, in my case, despite my best efforts, I was denied fairness. I was denied truth.

I had meetings. I sent letters. I made phone calls. I did everything I could to try and achieve justice. But in the end, justice was thwarted, not because of my lack of will or lack of justification, but because of the First Amendment of the Constitution. But I do not believe that the First Amendment was meant to be a legal loophole for an irresponsible press.

But for the past 7 years, a movement has been underway to help solve this injustice. The Uniform Correction Act (UCA) is currently being introduced to many state legislatures.

The UCA was written by the National Conference of Commissioners on Uniform State Laws, a group of legal experts appointed by state governments who have passed such legislation as the Uniform Commercial Code, the Uniform Gift to Minors Act and the uniform child support laws. The UCA laws are designed to establish a uniform process (around the nation) for correcting incorrect or potentially defamatory statements. The goal is to reduce litigation and gain vindication.

According to Richard Winfield, in "Correcting Errors May Equal Reducing Damages," (Editor and Publisher July 24, 1993),

> "An aggrieved target of a defamation gets a prompt and full correction and the prospect of reparation of actual economic loss. In return, the newspaper must publish a prompt and full correction to escape the possible ruinous prospect of paying punitive and reputational damages."

In Kentucky, we currently have laws governing "Libel actions against newspaper - demand for and publication of correction" which states,

> "In any action for damages for the publication of a defamatory statement in a daily or other newspaper the defendant shall be liable for actual damages sustained by plaintiff. The defendant may plead the publication of a correction in mitigation of damages. Punitive damages may be recovered only if the plaintiff shall allege and prove publication with legal malice and that the daily or other newspaper failed to make conspicuous and timely publica-

> tion of a correction after receiving a sufficient
> demand for correction."

However, after the significantly fabricated, wrongful front page, lead headline article against me, I wrote the reporter and various editors protesting the inaccuracies. No one at Gannett felt compelled to adhere to the Kentucky correction statute. Admittedly, I did not specifically send a written "sufficient demand for correction." However, if it is the constitutional obligation of the press to protect individual liberties, why did they not inform me of my right to send such a request?

But it may not have mattered anyway. Again, according to Richard Winfield,

> "About 30 states currently have retraction or
> correction statues on their books. For the most
> part, these statues are old, flawed and ineffec-
> tive. For example, most of these laws fail to
> provide a newspaper with a compelling legal
> reason to publish a correction."

Hence, unless the press has a legal incentive to correct wrongful misstatements against citizens, why do it?

Furthermore, according to Barbara W. Wall (vice president and - oddly enough - senior legal counsel of Gannett Co. Inc.), and Richard N. Winfield in "Uniform Correction Act goes to states for passage," (Editor and Publisher January 28, 1995),

> "At a practical level, most of the present
> correction laws are self-defeating. With good
> reason in many cases, editors have come to
> perceive the timely correction of misinforma-

tion as a dangerous admission of error that
might haunt their publication in a subsequent
libel suit. Thus, for fear of future costly
litigation, the correction of the offending act is
sometimes brushed aside."

Hence, although it might be the just thing to do, correcting libelous statements is often avoided simply to protect the financial bottom line of the newspaper.

Scary.

Furthermore, in the same article, it is stated,

"Although most libel suits are won by the
press, often on appeal, they are costly to all
parties in terms of money, time, effort, and
results. This situation is harmful to the press, the
plaintiff, and the public."

But why are most libel suits won by the press? And why on appeal? This is why I call for more judicial balance in favor of the individual liberties of citizens. I call for balance of what has become essentially a kangaroo court for the benefit of the multi-billion dollar press industry.

Because as it stands today, protecting irresponsible actions of the press have been given priority over protecting individual liberties. This is why passage of the UCA would be a Godsend to citizens such as myself, as well as to my reputation and family. The press would have been held more accountable, and I would have had the record set straight. Again, according to Barbara Wall and Richard Winfield,

"Thus, under the UCA, the news organization
that runs a legitimate correction wins a major
advantage: immunity from large damages. It

> may still face a suit, but the real hazard of a multimillion-dollar verdict is eliminated.
>
> The same holds true for the libel plaintiff: If he requests a correction, and shows that the story about him was wrong, he will be vindicated with a full, fair, and timely correction. The record will be set straight soon, which will help restore his reputation."

I think that passage of the UCA would have many potential benefits. First of all, it should be remembered that much of the momentum in passing this act is from those in the press, or those who represent the press, who feel that such an act would reduce libel law suits. Fairness to citizens is an added bonus.

Secondly, this act has also been carefully written to avoid constitutional infringements. Afterall, requiring the press to grant a "full, fair, and timely correction" could not reasonably be argued to impair the "freedom of the press." The only impairment that could conceivably occur would be if the press was shown to be repeatedly irresponsible, and was required to repeatedly publish corrections and apologies. In that case, readers would soon become even more cynical about the accuracy of what they read, and the readership would probably erode even more quickly than they are today.

Sooner or later, two things would happen. First, readership of sloppy newspapers would decline to the point that the paper would have to shut down. Or, secondly, the editors would institute policy that insured accuracy in their reporting.

Either way, this would serve the intent of the Constitution.

Because individual liberties should never be dismantled, even by the press.

And the perspective of the story is never more important than the facts of the story.

CASE STUDY OF THE APPLICATION OF MY SUGGESTIONS

What would have occurred in my case if libel laws favored the citizen, and if the UCA was passed?

First of all, if the Gannett reporter and editors knew that deliberate misstatement of facts could result in a reasonable chance that I could be awarded loss of income, loss of reputation, and punitive damages, they would have been less likely to act with "actual malice." As such, I believe that the significantly fabricated, front page, lead headline article would never have been published.

However, if libel laws did favor the individual liberties of citizens, and the significantly fabricated story had been published, then I, as well as other citizens wrongfully harmed by such irresponsible reporting would have the ability to be awarded reasonable damages. As such, it would probably not take long for Gannett to decide that reporting the truth was not only in the best interests of the individual liberties of citizens, but also in the best interest of their financial existence.

Subsequently, the Gannett Courier-Journal would possibly rediscover their constitutional obligation to protect individual liberties, and rediscover that it is the dedication to report the truth that defines journalism as a profession.

But consider if the reporter had simply made a mistake. This clearly did not occur in my case, and no one at Gannett to this day has claimed that the deliberate, and significantly fabricated, front page, lead headline story was anything less than an attempt to discredit me because I am a doctor. But consider if this same story had appeared in a newspaper that valued truth in their reporting. And consider if it truly was a tragic mistake. In this case, The Uniform Correction or Clarification of Defamation Act would apply. (See Appendix)

According to Section 1, the blatantly false accusation that I charged "almost six times" the amount charged by the patient's previous doctor for "the same procedure" would have been defined as a "defamatory" statement, "tending to harm" my reputation.

According to Section 2, the Gannett Courier-Journal would have been held accountable to this law.

According to Section 3, I would have had within 90 days to submit a "timely and adequate request for correction or clarification" to the Gannett Courier-Journal.

According to Section 4, the Gannett Courier-Journal would have been entitled to ask me "to disclose reasonably available information material to the falsity of the allegedly defamatory statement." (However, in my case, the facts were clearly documented before the story. He simply chose to ignore the facts, and lied to the reader.)

According to Section 5, if a subsequent correction was made, I would then only be entitled to recover economic loss if I elected to proceed with litigation for libel. I would not be able to recover for claims of loss of reputation, and punitive damages.

According to Section 6, the Gannett Courier-Journal would have been required to publish the correction within 45 days after my request. Furthermore, the correction would have been "published with a prominence and in a manner and medium reasonably likely to reach substantially the same audience as the publication" of the misstatement. In other words, since the misstatements against me were on page one, the correction would have to have been on page one.

According to Section 7, if I did not feel that the correction was sufficient, I would have 20 days (more or less, depending on the state) to challenge the sufficiency.

According to Section 8, if the Gannett Courier-Journal elected not to publish the correction in a "timely" manner, and I pursued litigation, then they would have the opportunity to offer, "at any time before trial, to make a correction or clarification." In this case, the offer would be required to be made in writing. This agreement would include payment of my attorney fees, and a "copy of the proposed correction." If I accepted this settlement, I would be "barred from commencing an action against the publisher." Furthermore, if I did not accept this offer, I would be able to recover only "damages for provable economic loss, and reasonable expenses of litigation." Furthermore, at the request of the Gannett Courier-Journal or myself, the court could "determine the sufficiency of the offered correction or clarification."

According to Section 9, the protections granted to the Gannett Courier-Journal in such a settlement would not extend to anyone, or any institution that desired to republish the wrongful story.

According to Section 10, the request for correction or clarification, the contents of the request, and the acceptance or refusal of the request would not be admissible at trial.

Most folks would agree that the intent, as well as the provisions of the Uniform Correction Act are equally fair to both the press, and the citizen who has been libeled. Unfortunately, I haven't heard a great outcry from the press to champion this fair proposal. It is my suspicion that the press is not very interested in fairness.

Afterall, current libel laws are weighted far to the benefit of the press. So why rock the boat just for the sake of fairness - just for the sake of protecting a few individual liberties?

THE TEN RULES OF DEALING WITH AN IRRESPONSIBLE PRESS

Considering the enourmous power of the press, it may be some time before citizens are given equal footing in dealing with a press who enjoys, and is quite protective of their current minimal accountability status. As such, I hope that others can learn from the misstakes I made. Remember, it was I who steadfastly believed that when it comes to reporting the news, I had faith that reporters and editors had an uncompromising dedication to truth, and have an unyielding respect and compassion for the reputation of the very citizens they have a constitutional obligation to protect.

It was I who got kicked in the teeth.

It was I who was naive.

Therefore, I have ten suggestions that I think everyone should know when dealing with an accusation by the press.

They are:

THE TEN RULES OF DEALING WITH AN IRRESPONSIBLE PRESS

(1) Know "The Ten Rules of the 90' Press."

(2) When confronted with an allegation, ask the reporter to specifically state the accusation.

(3) Do not immediately comment on any accusation by a reporter.

(4) Seek counsel and avoid lengthy discussions with the reporter, regardless of your lack of involvement or innocence.

(5) Meet with the reporter's editor before the story is published if you know, or you feel the reporter to be irresponsible.

(6) Keep meticulous records.

(7) If after the story is published, you have been libeled, write the reporter and editor immediately, and demand a retraction.

(8) Also, contact the ombudsman, or whoever deals with public complaints.

(9) If the press refuses to make the appropriate corrections or retractions, then inquire as to your state libel laws, and inquire as to if the UCA has been passed into law in your state.

(10) Try to accept that under current libel laws, reputation is worthless.

(1) Know "The Ten Rules of the 90's Press

As an Endocrinologist, researcher, comic, musician, and janitor, my career has focused on how things work. I have always been fascinated by systems. Because of my past success in dealing with such systems, I thought I would reasonably be able to deal with the press. Unfortunately, I made a grave error in believing that it was the dedication to reporting the truth that defined journalism as a profession. As such, I grossly miscalculated the appropriate mechanistic approach to the reporter, and paid the price. In retrospect, I wish I would have been warned of how the press is not only able, but willing to use their privileged power to dismantle individual liberties.

(2) When confronted with an allegation, ask the reporter to specifically state the accusation.

When I first spoke to the reporter, it is likely he had already written most of the story, based solely on the information provided by the accuser. When he called to ask for a last minute input from me (the accused), he was obviously taken off guard by the facts - because the facts did not fulfill his "perspective." Hence, he was required to repeatedly change his story premise until he found one that he could reasonably fabricate. In retrospect, I should have asked for the specific accusation up front. Subsequently, I should have limited all further comment to that issue only. I should not have allowed him the opportunity to "fish" for a story.

(3) Do not immediately comment on any accusaton by a reporter.

This was not a breaking story. Yet the Gannett reporter employed "bully tactics" to force me to respond before having the opportunity to get, and review the facts. In retrospect, my second response to the reporter (after obtaining the specific accusation) should have been to demand the opportunity to review the records before responding.

(4) Seek counsel and avoid lengthy discussions with the reporter, regardless of your lack of involvement or innocence.

It was my feeling that the more facts provided to the reporter, the more obligated he would be to present the facts, and the greater the chances the story would be a non-story, and it would die. However, I now recognize that once a reporter and his editors have a "perspective," the story will be published, regardless of the merits of the story, or the potential harm to reputation or family of the accused. As such, my extensive discussion with the reporter only served to fill the body of the text, and only served to have my name mentioned 11 times in an isolated billing dispute that occured over two years prior at another medical practice. Those physicians who did not respond had their name listed only once, if at all.

I should have kept my mouth shut.

(5) Meet with the reporter's editor before the story is published if you know, or you feel, the reporter to be irresponsible.

This was one of only two things I did that I felt was wise. I believe that when I met with the editor in the presense of the reporter, I had a witness that the reporter knew the truth before the story was published. In this meeting, the reporter assured me he would report the truth about the relative charges. He also assured me that the story had nothing to do with doctor's pay. Both would prove to be lies. So even though my meeting did not insure truth or fairness, I do gain some satisfaction in knowing that an editor at the Gannett Courier-Journal, Gideon Gill, knows the truth. And considering that it was he who gave me his assurance that he would not allow anything to be reported unless it was fair to me and fair to doctors, and considering that it was he who failed to respond to my letter after the story...well...I hope he sleeps well at night.

And by the way, if you do have such a meeting, bring a tape-recorder. You can bet they will.

(6) Keep meticulous records.

This was the second thing I did that I felt was wise. I kept copies of all letters, faxes, as well as detailed logs of phone conversations. Furthermore, I sent a letter to the Gannett reporter asking him to confirm that he had received all my other letters. Many of these letters are quoted in this book. And since the Gannett reporter acknowledged that he received these letters, he cannot reasonably claim that he was not provided the facts. Nor can he claim that he misunderstood the facts. And if after the story was published, I had presented this documentation to an editor committed to reporting the truth, I think it would have mattered. The bottom-line is, if you do choose to respond to a reporter, be sure your response is documented, in writing, or recorded.

(7) If after the story is published, you have been libeled, write the reporter and editor immediately, and demand a retraction.

After the wrongful story against me, I sent numerous letters of protest. However, I did not specifically ask for a retraction. I again assumed that if the editors knew that the reporter deliberately fabricated the story, they would take it upon themselves to correct the problem, and make amends. And I must admit believing the lead editor and vice president of the Gannett Courier-Journal when he agreed (after asking "What can we do?"), that he would have someone at Gannett to inquire as to my volunteer efforts with the homeless, as well as my medical research. Neither occurred. And when I asked my attorney to insist on a correction, he stated "You can't expect to tell the press what to print." Therefore, to this day, many people in the state of Kentucky think that I overcharge patients. They do not know the facts. They only know the fabricated fantasies of an irresponsible Gannett reporter, supported and encouraged by his editors.

(8) Also, contact the ombudsman, or whoever deals with public complaints.

After the wrongful story against me, I contacted the ombudsman. Instead of a response, I received a threat from the Gannett attorney. Nevertheless, since the ombudsman for the Gannett Courier-Journal has been known to responsibly correct misleading or inaccurate reporting, it is probably worth the time to pursue.

Another potential option is to personally meet with the editors after a libelous story. This may be of some benefit. But remember, these meetings often end with the editor making promises of atonement that aren't kept, and making stock assurances that he/she will "make every effort to ensure that any such future problems do not happen again." And while as the editor may benefit from the educational experience of discussing your complex situation, the only benefit you will likely receive will be a "feel good" impression that the pain you and your family experienced somehow really mattered to the press.

So meet afterwards if you must. But be assured, if you are personally, or professionally, associated with one of the subjects on the press' "mounting" list (see text), nothing will prevent future harmful stories against you, your profession, or your situation.

(9) If the press refuses to make the appropriate corrections or retractions, then inquire as to your state libel laws, and inquire as to if the UCA has been passed in your state.

Also, if you do seek counsel, be sure that it is an attorney with substantial experience with libel cases in your state.

(10) Try to accept that under current libel laws, your reputation is worthless.

We live in an uncertain time in American history where we, as a nation, are looking inward to seek and demand greater discipline from ourselves, as well as others. We are growing to understand that accountability and responsibility are required of all of us.

Furthermore, we are also coming to understand that money isn't everything. America has enormous financial resources. But despite the huge monetary wealth, we all know, in our bones, that something is lacking. We have overvalued materialism, and undervalued character.

This is why I am so fascinated, and confused about the emphasis of current libel laws. If a citizen is clearly shown to have been the victim of an irresponsible press (who has acted with "actual malice"), the Supreme Court decisions have made it very difficult for citizens to win judgements concerning dismantling of individual liberties. Therefore, it is too often that the only claims that have a prayer of success involve loss of income. And even those judgements found in favor of citizens are often overturned on appeal.

In a time in America when we are trying to emphasize character (and thus reputation) over materialism (income), I find it disturbing that our judicial system feels that only loss of income is worthy of recovery.

Punitive damages against an irresponsible press who engages in the systematic dismantling of individual liberties is,

"Inappropriate."

And loss of reputation is worthless.

THE PERSPECTIVE

AFTERWORD

As can probably be discerned from my discussion, I am a citizen who is disillusioned about the integrity of the press. And my disillusionment is not based on opinion, it is based on experience.

In my case, a two year old, isolated billing complaint (1) that occurred while as an employee at another medical practice, (2) that was resolved with a refund, and (3) that originated from a woman known to "change doctors as often as some people change hairdressers," was deemed of such journalistic merit as to warrant a front page, lead headline story of the day.

Furthermore, for the purpose of creating a "perspective," the reporter lied to the reader about the facts of the story, lied to me about the purpose of the story, and lied to his own editor as to when he notified me of the story.

As a result, my reputation and family were wrongfully harmed.

Afterward, the editors refused to grant atonement, despite giving me the most sacred of assurances - they gave me their word. Instead, I received a threatening letter from a Gannett attorney.

In the process of trying to achieve justice, I discovered that the very Bill of Rights that was intended to protect individual liberties, was successfully used by the press as a legal loophole to dismantle individual liberties. The First Amendment meant nothing more than the creation of a great wall that separates the press' promotion of self-serving "perspectives" and financial priorities, from their constitutional obligation of reporting the truth, and honoring individual rights. Because of Supreme Court rulings, I found that the press was not reasonably accountable, and thus, not reasonably responsible.

I know that somewhere in America, there are a few lonely, brave members of the press who know this kind of journalism to be wrong. And to those in the press who believe that it is the dedication to protecting individual liberties through reporting the truth that defines journalism as a profession, I wish you good luck and God's speed in your efforts to ensure a more responsible press, and towards your ultimate goal of improving the individual's life, liberty, and pursuit of happiness.

APPENDIX

UNIFORM CORRECTION OR CLARIFICATION OF DEFAMATION ACT

The Uniform Correction Act (UCA) was drafted by The National Conference of Commissioners on Uniform State Laws during its annual conference meeting in 1993. At the time of this writing, the act had been passed by only one state - North Dakota.

According to the prefatory notes of the draft, the stated purpose of this act was to help the courts to "achieve the proper balance between the constitutionally protected guarantees of free expression and the need to protect citizens from reputational harm."

Because of Supreme Court interpretations of the First Amendment, litigation to achieve justice regarding acts of defamation are complex, expensive, and often unrewarding. But, according to the prefatory notes, "unlike personal injuries harm to reputation can often be cured by other than money damages. The correction or clarification of a public defamation may restore the person's reputation more quickly and more thoroughly than a victorious conclusion to a lawsuit."

Furthermore, the sooner the correction is published, the greater the "the salutary effects of a correctional clarification are enhanced."

Unfortunately, under the current laws of resolving acts of libel or defamation, even if the courts find in favor of the injured or defamed plaintiff, the vindication often occurs long after the date of the initial injury. The damage has been done, often to the point of irreversible damage to reputation.

Many states have existing retraction statutes. However, according to the prefatory notes, they are "largely ineffective because they most often apply to a narrow range of cases and they do not create sufficient incentives on both parties, the plaintiff and defendant, can come to an agreement regarding retraction. Even the term retraction carries with it an implication of admission of wrong-doing, although in many instances the reputational harm arises from an interpretation not intended by the publisher or the publication of a reasonably believable information that subsequently turns out to be false."

The Uniform Correction or Clarification of Defamation Act provides incentives that, according to the prefatory notes, allow both the defendant, and the injured (defamed) party to correct or clarify an alleged defamation as an alternative to costly litigation." Furthermore, the Act "applies to all defamation, whether public or private, media or non-media, thus establishing a simplified structure for the resolution of all disputes. Moreover, the Act will provide a uniform set of requirements that will ensure the national media a consistent meaningful opportunity to correct or clarify."

UNIFORM CORRECTION OR CLARIFICATION OF DEFAMATION ACT

(Provided by the Secretary of State Alvin A Jaeger, State of North Dakota. It should be noted that the Act was approved by the Governor Edward T. Schafer on April 5, 1995 after a vote of 48 yeas, 0 Nays, in the state Senate, and 96 Yeas, 0 Nays in the State House)

FIFTY-FOURTH LEGISLATIVE ASSEMBLY STATE OF NORTH DAKOTA, BEGUN IN THE CAPITOL IN THE CITY OF BISMARCK, ON TUESDAY, THE THIRD DAY OF JANUARY, ONE THOUSAND NINE HUNDRED AND NINETY-FIVE.

SENATE BILL NO. 2101

- (JUDICIARY COMMITTEE)
- (AT THE REQUEST OF THE COMMISSION ON UNIFORM STATE LAWS)

An ACT to adopt the Uniform Correction or Clarification of Defamation Act; and to repeal section 14-02-08 of the North Dakota Century Code, relating to libel suits against newspapers, reputational interests and rights of free expression are advanced.

BE IT ENACTED BY THE LEGISLATIVE ASSEMBLY OF NORTH DAKOTA:

SECTION 1. DEFINITIONS. In this Act:

(1) "Defamatory" means tending to harm reputation.

(2) "Economic loss" means special, pecuniary loss caused by a false and defamatory publication.

(3) "Person" means an individual, corporation, business trust, estate, trust, partnership, association, joint venture, or other legal or commercial entity. The term does not include a government or governmental subdivision, agency, or instrumentality.

SECTION 2. SCOPE.

This Act applies to any claim or relief, however characterized, for damages arising out of harm to personal reputation caused by the false context of a publication that is published on or after the effective date of this Act. This Act applies to all publications, including writing, broadcasts, oral communications, electronic transmissions, or other forms of transmitting information.

SECTION 3. REQUEST FOR CORRECTION OR CLARIFICATION.

1. A person may maintain an action for defamation only if the person has made a timely and adequate request for correction or clarification from the defendant or the defendant has made a correction or clarification.

2. A request for correction or clarification is timely if made within the period of limitations for commencement of an action for defamation. However, a person who, within 90 days after knowledge of the publication, fails to make a good faith attempt to request a correction of clarification may recover only provable economic loss.

3. A request for correction or clarification is adequate if the request:

      a. Is made in writing and reasonably identifies the person making the request;

      b. Specified with particularity the statement alleged to be false and defamatory and, to the extent known, the time and place of publication;

      c. Alleges the defamatory meaning of the statement;

      d. Specifies the circumstances giving rise to any defamatory meaning of the statement which arises from other than express language of the publication; and

e. States that the alleged defamatory meaning of the statement is false.

4. In the absence of a previous adequate request, service of a summons and complaint stating a claim for relief for defamation and containing the information required in subsection 3 constitutes an adequate request for correction or clarification.

5. The period of limitation for commencement of a defamatory action is tolled during the period allowed in section 6 for responding to a request for correction or clarification. avoids the preclusive effective and inadequate earlier request for failure to seek a correction or clarification for any other reason.

SECTION 4. DISCLOSURE OF EVIDENCE OF FALSITY.

A person who has been requested to make a correction or clarification may ask the registrar to disclose reasonably available information material to the falsity of the alleged defamatory statement. If a correction or clarification is not made, a person who unreasonably fails to disclose the information after a request to do so may recover only provable economic loss. A correction or clarification is timely if published within twenty-five days after receipt of information disclosed under this section, or forty-five days after receipt of a request for correction or clarification, which ever is later.

SECTION 5. EFFECT OF CORRECTION OR CLARIFICATION.

If a timely and sufficient correction or clarification is made, a person may recover only provable economic loss, as mitigated by the correction or clarification.

SECTION 6. TIMELY AND SUFFICIENT CORRECTION OR CLARIFICATION.

1. A correction or clarification is timely if it is published before, or within forty-five days after, receipt of a request for correction or clarification, unless the period is extended under Section 4 of this Act.

2. A correction or clarification is sufficient if it:

    a. Is published with a prominent and in a manner and medium reasonably likely to reach substantially the same audience as the publication complained of;

    b. Refers to the statement being corrected or clarified and;

        (1) Corrects the statement;

        (2) In a case of defamatory meaning arising from other than the express language of the publication, disclaims an intent to communicate that meaning or to assert it's truth; or

(3) In the case of a statement attributed to another person, identifies the person and disclaims an intent to assert the truth of the statement; and

(c) Is communicated to the person who has made the request for correction or clarification.

(3) A correction or clarification is published in a medium reasonably likely to reach substantially the same audience as the publication complained of, if it is published in a later issue, edition, or broadcast of the original publication.

(4) If a later issue, edition, or broadcast or the original publication will not be published within the time limits established for a timely correction or clarification, a correction or clarification is published in a manner and medium reasonably likely to reach substantially the same audience as the publication complained of if:

a. It is timely and published in a reasonably prominent manner in another medium likely to reach an audience reasonably equivalent to the original publication or if the parties cannot agree on another medium, in the newspaper with the largest general circulation in the region in which the original publication was distributed;

b. Reasonable steps are taken to correct undistributed copies of the original publication, if any; and

c. It is published in the next practicable issue, edition, or broadcast, if any, of the original publication.

5. A correction or clarification is timely and sufficient if the parties agree in writing that it is timely and sufficient.

SECTION 7. CHALLENGES TO CORRECTION OR CLARIFICATION OR TO REQUEST FOR CORRECTION OR CLARIFICATION.

(1) If a defendant in an action governed by this Act intends to rely on a timely and sufficient correction or clarification, the defendant's intention to do so, and the correction or clarification relied upon, must be set forth in notice served on the plaintiff within sixty days after service of the summons and complaint or ten days after the correction or clarification is made, which ever is latter. A correction or clarification is deemed to be timely and sufficient unless the plaintiff challenges it's time limits or sufficiency within twenty days after the notice is served.

(2) If a defendant in an action governed by this Act intends to challenge the adequacy or timeliness of a request for correction or clarification, the defendant must set forth

the challenge in a motion to declare the request inadequate or untimely serve within sixty days after service of the [summons and complaint]. The court shall rule on the motion at the earliest appropriate time before trial.

SECTION 8. OFFER TO CORRECT OR CLARIFY.

1. If a timely correction or clarification is no longer possible, the publisher of an alleged defamatory statement may offer, at any time before trial, to make a correction or clarification. The offer must be made in writing to the person allegedly defamed by the publication and :

    a. Contain the publishers offer to publish, at the person's request, a sufficient correction or clarification; and pay the person's reasonable expenses of litigation, including attorney fees, incurred before publication of the correction or clarifications; and be accompanied by a copy of the proposed correction or clarification and the plan for it's publication.

2. If the person accepts in writing an offer to correct or clarify made pursuant to subsection 1, the person is barred from commencing an action against the publisher based on the statement or if an action has been commenced, the court shall dismiss the action against the defendant with prejudice after the defendant complies with the terms of the offer.

3. A person who does not accept an offer made in

conformance with subsection 1 may recover in an action based on the statement only damages for provable economic loss and reasonable expenses of litigation, including attorney fees, incurred before the offer, unless the person failed to make a good faith attempt to request a correction or clarification in accordance with subsection 2 of section 3 of this Act or failed to disclose information in accordance with Section 4 of this Act.

4. On request of either party, a court shall properly determine the sufficiency of the ordered correction or clarification.

5. The court shall determine the amount of reasonable expenses of the litigation, including attorney fees, specified in subsections 1 and 3.

SECTION 9. SCOPE OF PRODUCTION.

A timely and sufficient correction or clarification made by a person responsible for a publication constitutes a correction or clarification made by all persons responsible for that publication other than a republisher. However, a correction or clarification that is sufficient only because of the operation of Section 6(b)(2)(iii) does not constitute a correction or clarification made by the person to whom the statement is attributed.

SECTION 10. ADMISSIBILITY OF EVIDENCE OF CORRECTION OR CLARIFICATION.

1. The fact for correction or clarification under this

Act, the content of the request, and it's acceptance or refusal are not admissible in evidence at trial.

2. The fact that a correction or clarification under this [Act] was made and the contents of the correction or clarification are not admissible in evidence at trial except in mitigation of damages pursuant to Section 5. If the fact that a correction or clarification was made or the contents of the correction or clarification are received in evidence, the fact of the request may be received.

3. The fact of an offer of correction or clarification, or the fact of it's refusal, and the contents of the offer are not admissible in evidence of trial.

SECTION 11. REPEAL

Section 14-02-08 of the North Dakota Century Code is repealed.

THE PERSPECTIVE

THE STORY

THE FOLLOWING IS THE TEXT OF THE FRONT PAGE, LEAD
HEADLINE STORY OF THE GANNETT COURIER-JOURNAL
JUNE 4, 1995

- *(ACCOMPANIED BY HELPFUL "NOTES" THAT
  REPRESENT POTENTIAL THOUGHT PROCESSES OF
  THE REPORTER).**

Woman changes doctors, almost triples her bill.

- *[Reporter's notes: "Doctors are greedy bastards."]*

By   PATRICK   HOWINGTON
Staff Writer

Ms. E.C. has gotten the same medical tests
every year since her thyroid was removed in
1955. She sees a doctor each year to make
sure the dosage of her thyroid medicine is
right.

Most years her visit to the doctor and lab
work cost about the same, because she has
the same things done. The cost has crept up
with inflation, topping $100 in the 1990's.

But two years ago, her bill skyrocketed - to
almost $400.

The endocrinologist she went to that year
charged her $200 for the office visit, almost
six times the $35 that an internist had
charged her the year before. After she
complained, the endocrinologist reduced the
fee to $97.

300

● *[Reporter's notes: "Sure this $200 versus $35 charge is blatantly inaccurate. But intentionally fabricating facts is a valuable reporting technique. Please note how I cleverly divided the numbers to give the effect of accuracy. So yes, I may have deliberately lied to the reader, but how can a reporter create his perspective unless he has the courage to deceive?"]*

His office, EA, also charged her $179 for laboratory tests. That was twice as much as the $90 she had paid the previous year to have the same tests done - by the same local lab.

Including $6 for drawing the blood, Ms. E.C.'s bill for her February 1992 visit came to $385.

"When I first got the bill, I honesty thought it was a mistake. I thought they had put down the charges twice," said Ms. E.C., 60, of Louisville.

Ms. E.C.'s experience shows two things about our health care system: Doctors have a lot of leeway in what they charge, and patients don't have much knowledge about or much control over those charges.

● *[Reporter's notes: "The free enterprise system should not apply to doctors. They are greedy bastards."]*

After getting the bill, Ms. E.C called EA, a respected medical practice in downtown Louisville. She was assured that the fees she was charged were "the usual fees for an area endocrinologist," she said.

Ms. E.C. is an intelligent woman, a former literature professor with a Ph. D. who runs an information-systems business. She knew that seeing an endocrinologist - specialist in endocrine glands, including the thyroid - would cost more than going to an internist.

- *[Reporter's notes: "Anyone with a Ph. D. is an intelligent person. Anyone with an M.D. is a greedy bastard."]*

But not that much more, She decided to protest. She fired off a letter to the Jefferson County Medical Society and sent a copy to EA.

- *[Reporter's notes: "Yeah, she fired a letter! Someone has to stop these greedy bastards.]*

The doctor who had examined her, Harold Bays, told the medical society that his charge for the in-depth exam was appropriate. He later agreed, however to reduce Ms. E.C.'s office-visit fee to $97. Ms. E.C. settled her account, and switched doctors.

- *[Reporter's notes: "Well yes, the account was settled over two years before. But doctors are greedy bastards."]*

TELL US YOUR EXPERIENCE

Do you have an example of medical spending you consider unnecessarily high? If so, please call (---) --- - ---- and speak to Patrick Howington or leave a message.

- *[Reproter's notes: "Do you have an injury? My brother-in-law is an attorney.]*

DOCTOR'S PAY

Median 1992 income of some types of physicians. "Median" means half the physicians in each group made more than the amount listed, and half made less. According to the American Medical Association, the median income for all physicians in 1992 was $148,000.

Family practitioners $112,585

Pediatricians $116,637

Internists $119,538

Psychiatrists $120,000

Endocrinologists $123,516

Neurologists $153,140

Oncologists $167,406

General surgeons. $187,073

Plastic surgeons $197,500

Ophthalmologists $199,183

Obstetricians, gynecologists . . . $206,133

Urologists $215,721

Anesthesiologists $235,000

Cardiologists (non-invasive) . . . $243,912

Hand surgeons $260,903

Radiologists $271,723

Orthopedic surgeons. $289,323

Cardiologists (invasive). $320,476

Neurosurgeons $383,572

Heart surgeons $499,901

● *[Reporter's notes: "Yes, I may have deliberately mislead the reader about Dr. Bays' actual pay and yes, I may have deliberately lied to Dr. Bays when I assured him that this article would have nothing to do with doctor's pay, but how can a reporter create his perspective unless he is willing to deceive?"]*

Bays, who left EA in mid-1992 to form his own practice, said he was not a partner of that group and had no say over its fee schedule or what it charged for lab work..,

● *[Reporter's note: "Any business arrangement that generates any income to doctors must be corrupt, regardless of the potential savings to patients. Doctors should not make money from taking care of sick people. Doctors are greedy bastards."]*

As for the office-visit charge, Ms. E.C. thought she knew what to expect, having seen many doctors for her condition. She is a picky consumer and changes doctors as often as some people change hairdressers.

● *[Reporter's note: "Typical woman. She also probably owns too many shoes and can't read a road map."]*

She figured an endocrinologist would charge a little more, especially for a first visit when the doctor would need to take her full history. But, like most people, she didn't ask about the group's charges when she made the appointment.

● *[Reporter's note: "Well, maybe 'most' people really do ask for the charges. But doctors are greedy bastards."]*

Even if she had asked, Ms. E.C could have been quoted just a price range, because charges are based partly on how complex the doctor rates an exam.

Bays called her exam "highly complex," for two reasons. First, the case was medically complex - Ms. E.C. was on allergy drugs that, combined with her thyroid medicine, could cause problems. Second, he said, E.C. was highly argumentative, resisting his advice to diet and exercise - prolonging the visit and making it unpleasant.

● *[Reporter's note: "She was probably just upset because of a bad hair day - which is why she needed to go to all those hairdressers."]*

E.C. said she wasn't overly argumentative but asked Bays to focus just on her thyroid condition. Other than that, she wasn't upset about the quality of care she received.

Bays said the bill also was about $25 to $50 higher because he mistakenly thought that the doctor who recommended EA - her allergist - was consulting him on her condition. So Bays sent him a three-page letter of his findings, billing for writing and dictation time.

After reviewing his records, Bays said another mistake might have occurred. Noting that his response to the medical society called the office visit "moderately complex," he said he may have just mismarked Ms. E.C.'s charge, which he resolved by lowering the fee to $97.

Bays' letter to the medical society, however, made no mention of a billing error. Nor had anyone at EA suggested that when Ms. E.C. called to contest the bill.

● *[Reporter's note: "I know this he said / she said yarn about an isolated, two year old, billing dispute appears to be going absolutely nowhere. But hopefully, people are getting the general sense that doctors are greedy bastards."]*

Bays said it was ironic that his name would be in a story about a high bill. In his new practice, he said, he has never charged a patient for a "highly complex" [office] visit, and an insurance plan found his costs of treating patients were lower than most doctor's costs. He said he also saves patients money by stressing prevention, and that his income is less than the norm for endocrinologists.

Bays also said he was justified in charging more than E.C.'s internist for an office visit because of the expertise gained from his extra two years of training in endocrinology and the extra time he spends to counsel patients.

None of that - not even the reduced fee - mollified Ms. E.C., who said it was principle that counted.

"It (never was) a matter of money," she said.

● *[Reporter's notes: "It was always a matter of money."]*

"It was the unfairness of being charged (three times as much for) the same procedure," including "exactly the same tests by exactly the same laboratory."

● *[Reporter's notes: "Well, yes, the 45 - 60 minute complex exam with a three page letter by Dr. Bays was really not the "exact same procedure" as the quick 10 minute thyroid medicine refill by the previous doctor. But doctors are greedy bastards."]*

* The name of the patient, and of my previous practice has
been abbreviated for this book. Their names were included
in the original story.

Also, after the story was published, I wrote to the reporter,
various editors, and the ombudsman of the Gannett Courier
Journal. They declined to return my inquiries. To this day, I
still do not know why the reporter deliberately lied to the
reader about the facts, lied to me about the content of the
story (with regard to doctor's pay), and lied to his editor as
to when I was first notified of the story. Therefore, the
"Reporter's notes" are my "best guess" interpretations of
what may have been going on in the mind of this Gannett
reporter.

THE PERSPECTIVE

REFERENCES

Axelrod A, Phillips C. "What Every American Should Know About American History. 1992 Bob Adams Inc.

Bloomberg Business News/ProQuest - The New York Times (R) Ondisc. "Company reports: Gannett Co." Oct. 12, 1994: New York Times

Budiansky, S "The Media's Message - The public thinks the national press is elitist, insensitive and arrogant." January 9, 1995: U.S. News and World Report

Gannon, JP "A Fight for the Soul of Newspapers - Sensationalism and Gimmicks are Overtaking Responsibility. July 24, 1994: Courier Journal

Hawpe, DV "Hyper-Journalism vs. The Public Interest" February 21, 1993: Courier Journal

Lewis, A "Make No Law: The Sullivan Case and the First Amendment" 1991: New York Times Co.

REFERENCES

Monk LR. "The Bill of Rights - A User's Guide." 1991 Closeup Foundation

U.S. Department of Labor Bureau of Labor Statistics. "Occupational Outlook Handbook." 1994 - 1995 Edition

....

Uniform Correction or Clarification of Defamation Act. Drafted by the National Conference of Commissioners on Uniform State Laws. Approved and Recommended for Enactment in all the States at its Annual Conference Meeting in its One-Hundred-And-Second Year in Charleston, South Carolina July 30 - August 6, 1993

ABOUT THE AUTHOR

Health care reform has received much attention in the past several years. But one perspective has been ignored - a comic's perspective.

Dr. Harold Bays is an educator, researcher and has been the featured speaker for numerous academic and other medical programs and symposia. As the only stand-up Endocrinologist in the world, he has performed at top comedy clubs around the country since 1987.

Since 1989, Dr. Bays has combined his comedy skills with his medical experiences to raise tens of thousands of dollars to benefit patients with chronic diseases (such as cancer, arthritis and AIDS), the homeless, the United Negro College Fund, as well as other charities. He is probably best known as the featured comic of the "Stand Up Diabetes" program that has taken him around the nation to raise funds for the American Diabetes Association and to increase awareness of this misunderstood disorder.

Dr. Bays first entered into comedy after being a professional musician (jazz, blues, and "60's" bands), busboy, dishwasher, cook, janitor, and clerk. His life's successes and failures have given him a unique political perspective on the issues of our times. He also has some comments about the state of medicine today.

On a professional level, Dr. Bays is the recipient of several medical academic awards, is Board Certified in Internal Medicine and in Endocrinology and Metabolism, is the Medical Director of a research center (conducting phase II-IV clinical research trials in new cholesterol and diabetes treatments), is a practicing Endocrinologist, is an Assistant Clinical Professor of the Department of Endocrinology and Metabolism at The University of Louisville School of Medicine, and has been elected as a Fellow of the American College of Physicians. He has published many world-wide medical articles on metabolic diseases such as "Diabetic Neuropathy" in Medical Clinics of North America and "Drug Treatment of Dyslipidemias" in the American Heart Association journal Heart Disease and Stroke. He is also an official medical consultant to the American Medical Association publication DRUG EVALUATIONS, a guide to state-of-the-art drug usage.

Dr. Bays has been "recognized with honor for his contributions to the medical profession and to the health and well being of the community at large" for his ongoing volunteer work with the homeless. He is also the distinguished, city-wide winner of the second annual Louisville "Kiss a Pig" fund raiser for the American Diabetes Association. Finally, Dr. Bays is involved in the development of a computer program that may revolutionize corporate medicine.

Dr. Bays' viewpoints may be controversial, but his perspective is unique, genuine, and suggests you don't have to be from the east or west coast to have an opinion.